Wisdom from Mi Madda

Jamaican Proverbs & Life Lessons

Anette Rose White

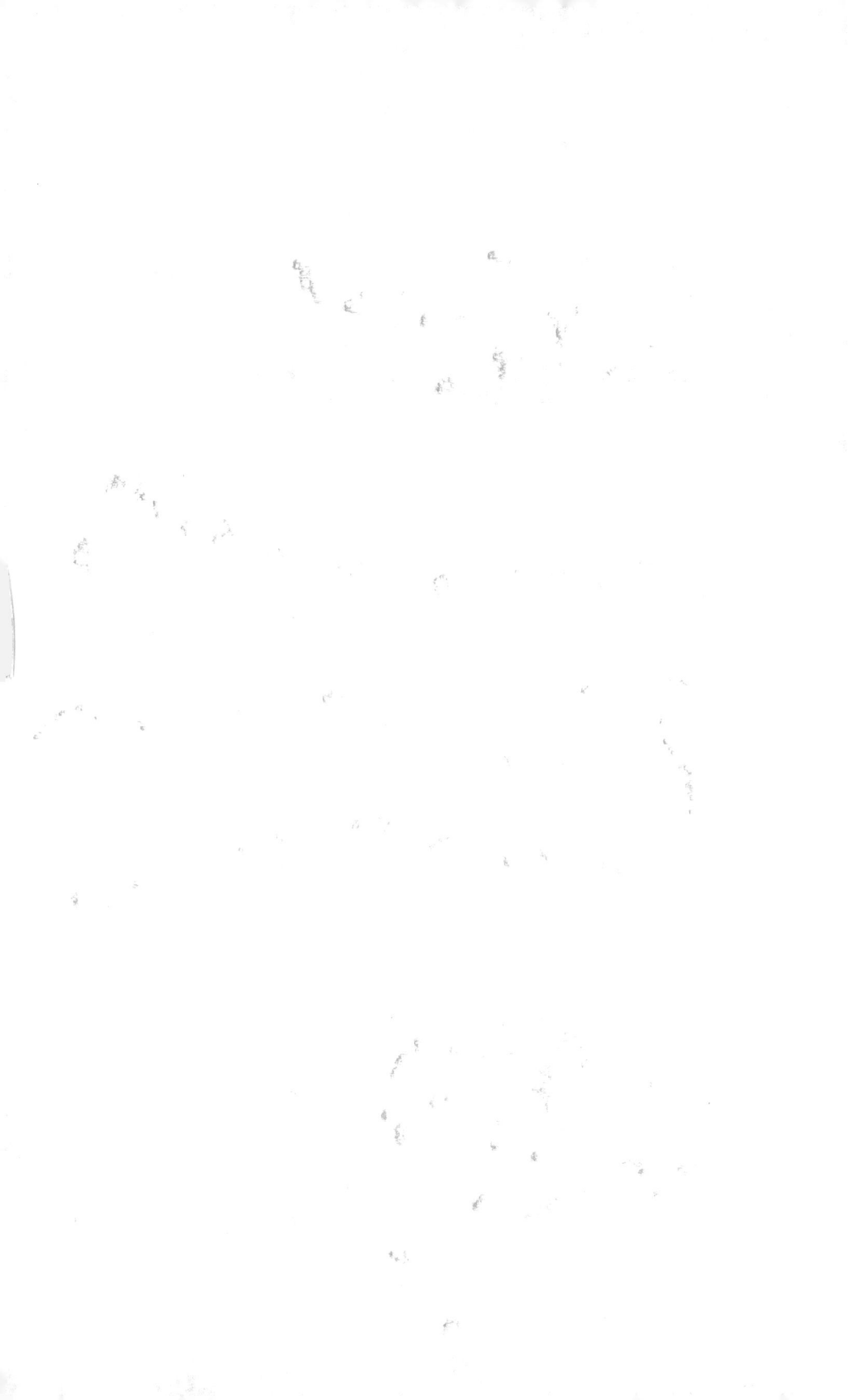

Copyright Page

Wisdom from Mi Madda

Copyright © 2025 by **Anette Rose White**

For permission requests, contact:

Anette White

[anette@anetter.com]

This work draws on Jamaican oral traditions, cultural proverbs, and personal storytelling. Some names, details, and circumstances have been adapted or changed to preserve privacy.

ISBN: 979-8-9932492-0-9

Printed in the United States of America

10 9 8 7 6 5 4 3 2 1

First Edition

Cover design by [Anette White]

Interior design by [Anette White]

Table of Contents

Dedication

To every madda who raised a generation with roots, reason, and reverence. Especially, my Madda

Gloria McPherson-Douglas

1930 – 1995 · Kingston, Jamaica

Matriarch, mentor, and the heartbeat of my every day, this volume is laid at your feet. You softened hardship with hymns, stretched small blessings like cloth over a table, and stitched proverbs into our pockets so we would never walk the world empty-handed.

From the zinc-roof mornings when you called us to prayer, to the lamp-lit nights when your stories braid history with hope, you modeled a scholar of the spirit: work hard, live honest, give thanks. Your kitchen was a classroom, your laughter a sanctuary, and your silence, when words would wound, an exercise in disciplined grace.

Mama Gloria, every page that follows bears the watermark of your wisdom: the rhythm of your tongue, the courage you taught by example, the compassion you practiced without fanfare. May these words stand as a small testament to the great legacy you left in hearts and habits.

Walk good, Mommy! Your light still finds us, steady as a bottle torch against the evening breeze.

Preface

Who Is Mi Madda?

Mi madda nuh live in no palace, but her presence? Royal. She ruled from a linoleum kitchen with a chipped enamel pot, a sharp tongue, and a tender touch. Her hands always busy, kneading flour, wringing out clothes, or pointing the way. Strong hands, rough from work, but gentle when smoothing hair or wiping tears. When she laugh, it come from her belly, wholehearted and loud, and when she vex, it was thunder before the rain.

She wore her strength quiet. Not the kind that shout, but the kind that stand firm when storm come. Mi madda teach without chalkboard. Every act was curriculum: how fi stretch rice, how fi carry yuhself like yuh name matter, how fi leave place better than yuh find it. She never quote book, but every word she seh stay in yuh memory like gospel: "Wash yuhmi foot before yuh lie down." "Mind yuh mouth." "Who cyan hear will feel." At the time, we thought it was irritating. Now? We know it was foundation.

She did not raise me alone. She raise neighborhood pickney, cousins passing through, and even grown men who only call when belly hungry or soul tired. She was mother in name, but matriarch in duty: part cook, part counselor, part compass. What she lacked in money, she made up in sense and spirit.

This book is her. Every line soaked in her tone, every proverb shaped by her way of reasoning. It nuh matter if she sit beside yuh now or just in memory: Mi Madda walk through these pages. She still remind yuh to say "Good mawnin," to cross yuh legs in public, and to never, ever borrow what yuh cyaan return.

Mi Madda might be one woman, but she represent many. She is yours too, if yuh ever know a woman who sacrifice quietly, who pray loud when she think nobody hearing, who stand in the gap when the system fail.

So read slow. Read with respect. And when yuh done, read again: not just with yuh eyes, but with yuh heart. Because Mi Madda's voice didn't retire when she passed. It echo in di wisdom we live and di legacy we carry forward.

Anette Rose White

Introduction

E very page of this book is braided with memory, my mother's voice in the early morning, her hands busy in the kitchen, her words sharp with truth or soft with grace. *Wisdom from Mi Madda* was born from the echoes of those moments, the kind that lingered long after the sound faded. It is a tribute not only to my mother, but to all the Jamaican women who taught with stories, led with proverbs, and raised children to be strong in spirit, sharp in mind, and rooted in values.

This book came to life during a season of reflection, on family, identity, and what it means to pass on wisdom in a world where voices are often drowned by noise. I began collecting the proverbs I grew up hearing, not just as cultural relics, but as everyday tools that helped me navigate life's challenges with dignity and resilience. I wanted my children, and yours, to inherit that same sense of direction.

But to truly hear *Mi Madda*, you must also hear Jamaica.

Jamaica's story is one of survival and strength. First inhabited by the Taíno people, then reshaped by Spanish conquest in 1494 and British colonization in 1655, the island became a hub of the transatlantic slave trade. Out of slavery and struggle rose resistance: the Maroons fled to the mountains and fought for freedom, ordinary people carved out dignity in markets and cane fields, and the nation carried forward a spirit of endurance. Jamaica gained independence in 1962, but long before then, its people had already claimed resilience as their birthright. Out of that history grew the sayings, songs, and stories that are the marrow of our culture.

Jamaican culture is not just lived, it is spoken, sung, and performed. Proverbs are as present in the kitchen as in the churchyard, as quick in a quarrel as in a comfort. They carry humor, rebuke, blessing, and warning, often in the same breath. To grow up Jamaican is to learn that wisdom can slip into a conversation like spice into a pot, subtle but unmistakable. *"One han' cyaan clap."* *"Rain a fall, but dutty tough."* *"Mi likkle but mi tallawah."* These are more than sayings; they are the code of survival and success.

The language of these proverbs is Jamaican patois, or Creole, a tongue born of necessity, defiance, and creativity. It bends English into rhythm and image, carrying echoes of West African languages, Spanish, and indigenous words. Jamaican patois is not broken English; it is a full, living language, rich in metaphor and music. Some truths simply cannot be translated without losing their fire. *"Cock mout kill cock"* hits sharper in patois than in English because it carries the cadence of a people who know that words can both build and destroy.

This book is organized thematically around the core elements of Jamaican upbringing:

- **Gratitude and Grounding** explores the moral and spiritual foundation passed on through simple yet profound sayings.

- **Grace Before Greatness** reflects the code of conduct our elders instilled in us from birth, where manners, humility, and self-respect were non-negotiable.

- **Wisdom in Proverbs** offers life lessons that span topics from patience to pride, from discernment to dignity.

- **Iron Sharpens Iron** highlights proverbs that encourage perseverance, discipline, and self-development.

- **Warnings and Wit** gathers the cautionary phrases that blend cultural critique with comedic clarity, reminding us to watch, listen, and learn.

- **Character, Connection, and Clarity** centers on how we speak, who we walk with, and the values that shape how we show up in the world.

- **Fate, Effort, and Consequence** unpacks how life unfolds, what we can control, what we must accept, and the price of our choices.

- **Wisdom in Action** emphasizes prudence, patience, and preparedness, showing how foresight and discipline help us weather storms and build resilience.

- **Life, Fate, and Human Nature** explores community, consequence, and survival, reminding us that loyalty, greed, kinship, and choice all shape the destiny we carry.

Whether you're 17 or 70, Jamaican by birth, heritage, or curiosity, this book meets you where you are, with just enough context for newcomers and deep resonance for those who grew up hearing these truths echo from veranda to church bench. Each proverb is paired with context, reflection, and real-life application. The tone is conversational but grounded, like sitting at your grandmother's table, where the stories come with side-eye and a sweet bun.

Whether you use this book as an educational resource, or simply to reconnect with our cultural roots, my hope is that it stirs memories, sparks conversations, and preserves the richness of our Jamaican heritage. This collection is not exhaustive, nor is it meant to fossilize our traditions. Instead, it invites us to reflect, remember, and reimagine how ancestral wisdom lives in us still, and how we might carry it forward with honor.

So, wherever you find yourself in the kitchen or classroom, diaspora or yard, open these pages and listen.

Because sometimes, all you need to move forward is one good word from *Mi Madda.*

Chapter 1

Gratitude and Grounding

G ratitude, faith, and moral grounding are the cornerstones of Jamaican upbringing. These values are passed down not only through sermons or schooling but through the everyday sayings of mothers, grandmothers, and wise elders who carry an answer for every situation. Whether you're high on hope or low on luck, there's always a proverb to steer you straight.

"Give thanks for what you have" is one of the first lessons many Jamaican children learn. It doesn't matter if dinner is dumpling and butter or a full spread, give thanks. This simple phrase encourages a mindset of contentment. It teaches that while ambition is good, ingratitude is not. As Granny would say while handing you the last piece of fried plantain, "Some people out dere don't even have dis." A young man might grumble about not landing his dream job, only to be reminded by his grandmother, "Yuh healthy and strong, enuh. Give thanks. Yuh time soon come."

"Belly full, man tell yuh say fasting good." This proverb means that people who are comfortable often give advice that ignores the real hardship of others. Jamaicans say it when someone who "nuh lack nothing" downplays the struggles of those who do.

It easy fi talk 'bout patience and sacrifice when yuh belly full. When yuh don't feel the pinch, yuh quick fi tell somebody else fi wait. But a hungry man don't want sermon, him want support. This reminds us that privilege can make yuh forget. It challenge yuh to stay humble, especially when yuh no longer in survival mode. Gratitude means remembering what it felt like to lack, even when yuh have more than enough.

"He who feels it knows it." Yuh cyaan dismiss a man suffering if yuh never carry di same weight. Mi madda would whisper dis when mi mock another person's hardship. Gratitude come when yuh remember yuh own rough road and extend mercy to others still walking theirs.

"Every mickle mek a muckle." In other words, don't despise small blessings. Whether it is a five-dollar raise or someone saving you a seat on the bus, it adds up. Like raindrops filling a barrel, small acts of grace and provision can create something mighty overtime. Jamaican mothers know this well, stretching meals, minutes, and money like magic.

"Tek kin teet cova heartburn." Sometimes laughter is the only shield. Gratitude mean finding joy even when yuh heart sore. Mi madda could lose a dollar at market and still joke on di walk home. Not because she nuh feel it, but because joy guard yuh spirit when circumstances rough. Gratitude nuh always come from plenty, sometimes it born from smiling through pain.

You laugh to keep from crying. Beneath the jokes and cheer might be grief, stress, or heartbreak. This proverb reminds us to look beyond the surface. Laughter is powerful, but so is empathy.

"Better belly buss than good food waste." This means it is better to have too much than to throw 'way blessings. From di kitchen to di classroom, this warn yuh: don't take anything for granted. Every plate of food represents work, farmers, cooks, parents, people who sacrifice. And food, like opportunity, nuffi throw 'way. Whether it is a chance, a gift, or a second helping; honor it. Because somewhere, somebody wish dem had it.

"Di dog with di bone lose di bone." This teaches the danger of greed and discontent. Jamaicans use it when someone loses what they had by reaching for more than they need.

The dog see him reflection, think it is another dog with another bone, and in trying to grab it, drop him own. Greedy people lose twice. Money, like magic, is a mirror fi those who always want more, even when dem already blessed. Gratitude remind yuh to stop chasing shadows and treasure what's in your hand.

So, when life gives you a little, treat it like much, and trust that more is on the way.

Next, there's the ever-present commandment: **"Pray."** In a Jamaican household, this isn't up for discussion. Prayer is not just a Sunday thing; it is a before-school, before-bed, before-yuh-eat, and before-you-make-any-big-decision kind of ritual. Even if yuh tief (steal), Granny might still say, "Mi hope yuh prayed before yuh pick up dat sin." Whether facing exams or a heartbreak, prayer grounds the soul and reminds you that you're never alone.

For some, it is the Lord's Prayer echoing off zinc-roof. For others, it is lighting a white candle and calling upon ancestors fi guidance. Rastafari might chant psalms or reason with Jah under the stars. And in Maroon traditions, drumming, herbs, and sacred words restore balance and clarity. Whether yuh speak to God, Jah, Spirit, or di Old People who walked before yuh, what matter most is dat yuh connect with something greater than self.

In moments of betrayal, disappointment, or injustice, the calm wisdom of **"Leave it to God"** often follows. Jamaicans trust divine timing. When someone wrongs you, there's no need to plot revenge. Your mother might say, "Leave it to God. Him always working, even when we cyan see." This is less about passivity and more about peace of mind. After all, vengeance takes energy, and that energy could be better spent minding your own business or making a good pot of soup.

This spiritual release, however, does not cancel the need for emotional discernment.

"Mi nuh eat from everybody kitchen." is about discernment, knowing that not every offer is good for you. Jamaicans use this to protect boundaries, spiritually and socially.

14

A meal might smell sweet but come with sour spirit. Some people serve smiles with bad mind. This saying isn't about being unkind, it is about being careful. Protect your energy. Not every invitation is a blessing. Know where yuh nourishment coming from, whether food, friendship, or favor.

Grace mus' walk hand-in-hand with good judgment.

"Dog that bring a bone carry one." The same person who whisper in yuh ear might be shouting yuh name somewhere else. This proverb remind yuh that gratitude also mean guarding yuh peace. Not everyone who comes with a story come with good intention. Be wise. The quieter yuh circle, the stronger yuh spirit.

"Rain nuh fall pon one man house." Trouble is no respecter of persons. Whether you're in a mansion or a board house, life will serve you hard days. This proverb reminds us to extend grace, because you never know when the next downpour will soak your roof.

"Every lizard lay down pon dem belly." It means that everyone may appear the same, but their experiences and struggles are not. Jamaicans say this to encourage empathy and understanding. Just because we all lying low don't mean we lying equal. One lizard's belly might be warm; another might be bruised.

This teach us not to judge someone just because dem look like dem managing. Gratitude grow when we stop comparing and start understanding. Your story is yours, nuh measure it against another man's.

Grounding yourself in empathy helps you carry your own storm with dignity and stand by others in theirs.

"Treat man good pan bottom." Anybody can show love when things and times are good. But when someone is at rock bottom, do you still see dem as worthy? This is about showing kindness, not convenience. It is a measure of true character. Life turns, today dem down, tomorrow dem up. The bridge yuh build with respect might be the same one yuh cross later. Gratitude isn't just about saying thanks, it is how yuh treat people when yuh don't "need" them.

"Forgive but don't forget." Mi madda seh it with both wisdom and warning. Forgiveness free yuh heart, but memory guard yuh steps. It's not about holding grudges. It's about learning the lesson without living in the wound.

"Dis day cyah hol' di nex." Meaning? Let today carry today's weight. Don't drag yesterday's pain into tomorrow's promise. After yuh forgive, let go. Because healing require both release and discipline, yuh cyah move forward with hands full of old hurt.

"Learn from your mistake" is a familiar refrain in Jamaican parenting. Make the wrong move and you'll get a talking-to, but not always a beating. Instead, expect a full sermon on what you did, why it was wrong, and how yuh mus' do better. Your missteps are meant to shape you. Fall once? Learn. Fall twice? Ahh, that leads us to the next point.

Then there's the quiet warning wrapped in poetic truth: **"Long run, short ketch."** You might think you're getting away with something, but sooner or later, consequences will catch up with you. Just ask the man who lie on every job application, he might land a big interview but wait 'til HR ask for references.

And finally, the reminder that no deed remains hidden: **"What is done in darkness will come to light."** Whether it is kindness or wrongdoing, truth will eventually reveal itself. Granny might not say a word when she notice you sneaking in late, but rest assured, when the time is right, she'll call your name with a tone that says she saw, and she knows. Actions echo, even in silence.

And sometimes, the truth isn't hidden; it is ignored. Like when someone warns you, but you brush it off until the storm hits. That's why Granny would say, **"If fish come from river bottom an' tell yuh say shark down deh, believe him."**

In other words, trust the voice of experience. Don't dismiss wisdom just because it comes from someone humble or quiet. If someone has walked the path, respect their insight, before you end up swimming with sharks of your own.

Not because it is all you deserve, but because it is a steppingstone, not a sentence. Contentment and ambition are not enemies; they're partners in the long run.

"No wait till drum beat before yuh grine yuh axe." Don't start preparing when the crisis hits; sharpen your skills, your spirit, your sense before the alarm sounds. Whether it is studying ahead of the exam or lying low before the gossip circle forms, readiness is a virtue. Jamaican grounding includes foresight.

"When man belly full, him tink a starvation time." Some people get so far from struggle, dem act like it never exist.

They talk like hardship is fiction, because dem not feeling it. This proverb humble yuh. It is a call to awareness. Comfort is a gift, not a license fi judge. Don't let your full belly make yuh forget the taste of hunger. Gratitude means memory. Memory means mercy.

Together, these proverbs form the moral compass of a Jamaican life well-lived. They balance reverence with realism, compassion with caution, and always, always, **faith with fire**. So, before you complain, lash out, or repeat that dumb move one more time, listen to the voices of the women who raised you. Chances are, they have already given you the wisdom you need.

Anette Rose White

Chapter 2

Grace Before Greatness

In Jamaica, manners are more than a formality; they're a way of life. You could be the brightest, best-dressed child in the room, but if you don't say "Good morning," the elders will look at you like you just committed a felony. Manners, along with good morals, are stitched into the fabric of a proper upbringing, and your parents will ensure you're fully hemmed before you leave the house.

First up, **"Be kind to others."** It sounds simple, but in Jamaican homes, this isn't optional. Kindness isn't just about smiling sweetly, it is helping yuh neighbor carry groceries, giving up your seat on the bus, or not bussin' a big laugh when somebody drop in public (even if it was funny). It is about choosing grace even when provoked. Your grandmother might say, "Don't meet bad wid bad. Kill dem wid kindness," while handing your rude cousin a piece of cake like nothing happened.

Right alongside kindness is the gold standard of upbringing: **"Kindness and good manners will get you through the world."** It is the Jamaican version of networking because who needs LinkedIn when a simple "Please" and "Thank you" could get you extra stew peas or even a job referral? In many stories, it is not the brightest student who gets the scholarship, but the one who showed respect to the right people along the way.

Then there's the ever relevant **"Do unto others as you would have them do to you."** This rule applies whether you're six years old sharing sweetie or sixty navigating office politics. Borrow a friend's car and return it clean, with gas. Otherwise, next time you ask, the keys will be "missing." Jamaicans believe strongly in fairness, reciprocity, and not taking kindness for weakness.

"Yuh cyah tek back spit." Words fling outta yuh mouth like stone, once dem drop, yuh cyah pick dem up. This proverb warn yuh: mind yuh speech, mind yuh attitude. Apologies are good, but some damage nuh fix with "sorry." In Jamaican homes, this saying teach children from early that every action have consequence. Grace before greatness mean thinking before yuh act, because not everything can be undone.

"Yuh cyah climb ladder wid han' inna yuh pocket." You rise by showing up, hands ready, heart willing. Whether you're helping others along the way or pulling your weight, success in Jamaica is tied to effort, not entitlement. This proverb reminds us: greatness and service walk hand in hand.

Graveyard full a people who feel important." Inna dis life, yuh haffi check yuh ego. Titles, applause, and position can fool yuh into thinking yuh irreplaceable, but di graveyard full a people who once thought so too. This proverb humble yuh. It remind yuh that greatness is not just about how high yuh climb, but how well yuh treat people along di way. When pride tek over, perspective get lost. True grace come from knowing that every blessing can be taken in a moment, so walk soft, and give thanks.

"Saying good morning to everyone who cross yuh path" is more than a simple greeting, it is a declaration that you were raised right. Walking into a room and not acknowledging others is a surefire way to get labeled as "bad bruk." Whether you're entering a taxi, passing someone on the street, or just stepping into a shop, a simple "Good morning" or "Good evening" is your passport to basic human decency.

"Respect your elders" isn't up for debate. In Jamaican homes, even a side-eye to your auntie can land you in deep trouble. You don't call grown people by their first name unless given express permission, and even then, you'd better add a "Miss" or "Mass" in front. Elders are treated with a level of reverence that borders on royalty, and woe be unto the child who forgets this hierarchy.

"Howdy and tenky nuh bruk no square." Manners never cost a cent, but them richer than gold. A simple greeting, a "thank you," can open doors pride would keep shut. People remember how you mek dem feel long after dem forget what you say. Gratitude and respect sweeten any space, and it mark you as somebody raised with values.

Courtesy opens doors, builds bridges, and preserves dignity, especially in small communities where your reputation often walks ahead of your résumé. You never know what a simple "Good evening" might open a door to or prevent.

"Children should be seen and not heard" is one of those proverbs that brings back memories of sitting at grown folks' tables in absolute silence, even though you had all the opinions in the world. Jamaican parents don't take kindly to "back chat," and jumping into adult conversation could earn you a quick glare, or worse, "the pinch under the table."

These days, some parents are shifting toward encouraging children to express themselves, but make no mistake, this proverb still echo strong in homes where respect is seen as the first stage of wisdom. It remind us that learning to listen is just as important as learning to speak.

"Stay outta big people business." If you've never heard this, you didn't grow up Jamaican. It is a phrase that comes flying at children who linger too long near adult conversations You could be minding your own business when suddenly you hear the grown folks talking on the verandah. You're tempted to linger, your ear tilted like a satellite dish, but don't. Big people business is sacred, dangerous, and strictly off-limits. Try eavesdropping, and your mother will remind you with one look that your ears don't belong in grown-up affairs.

"High seat kill Miss Thomas puss." Mi madda drop dis one whenever pride start creep in. It mean sometimes yuh run after position that too high, too heavy, and it crush yuh.

Ambition must walk wid humility. True greatness nuh require big chair, it require strong foundation.

"Mi come yah fi drink milk, mi nuh come fi count cow." Mi madda used dis proverb to teach restraint. It mean know your purpose. Yuh don't haffi destroy opportunity to enjoy it. Whether is job, friendship, or blessing, tek what offered with humility, don't overreach 'til yuh mash it up. Grace mean satisfaction, not greed.

"A soft answer turns away wrath." When tempers flare, cool heads prevail. A calm response has more power than a loud retort. This is the kind of grace that disarms enemies and diffuses tension. Jamaican wisdom tells us: speak truth but never lose your poise.

Also essential to this moral framework are two proverbial reminders about accountability. **"People who live in a glass house don't throw stone**." This cautions against hypocrisy. Before you judge someone, examine yourself. It is a call for humility in speech and conduct. Likewise, **"If yuh spit in the sky it will fall in yuh eye"** warns that bad intentions and careless words often rebound onto the one who casts them. In other words: think before you act or speak.

"Pig ask him mumma, 'Mumma, how yuh mouth suh long?' Mumma say, 'Wait, yuh time coming,." Translation: Youth have questions, but age has answers. You may not understand your parents' choices now but give them time. Live long enough, and you'll see the world from their view. This proverb affirms the deep patience of elders who know experience is the best teacher.

"Yuh cyah swear fi heart when face still smile." Don't be fooled by charm; discernment is part of wisdom. A person's smile may be genuine or a mask. Jamaican wisdom encourages you to look beneath the surface. Because in this culture, trust is earned, not assumed.

"Stick to yuh stick inna bush." Mean yuh fi stay loyal to who and what held you down before the spotlight come. This proverb is about remembering your roots, especially when new opportunities or temptations try fi pull yuh outta character. Mi madda used to say it when somebody switched up after a promotion or start treating old friends like strangers. Because true greatness isn't just about elevation, it is about who you remain loyal to on the way up. Dignity under pressure means not letting position erase principle. Stand firm. Shine bright, but don't forget who lit di candle when it was dark.

Together, these teachings form the social glue of Jamaican life. They instill respect, humility, and emotional intelligence, traits that, when applied properly, can take you far in life. Or at the very least, keep you out of trouble at family functions.

Wisdom From Mi Madda

Chapter 3

Wisdom in Proverbs

Jamaican wisdom has a rhythm all its own, sharp, witty, and often condensed into just a few words. These proverbs carry generations of lived experience, usually laced with humor and double meaning. They're not just things your grandmother says before she swats you with a dish towel; they're blueprints for how to survive, thrive, and sidestep the same trouble twice.

We begin with a classic: **"One-one coco full basket."** This saying is an anthem of patience and perseverance. It reminds us that success don't come overnight. Whether yuh saving money, studying for exams, or rebuilding yuh life, it is the small, consistent efforts that make the difference. Like Aunt Merle, who sold patties one at a time for twenty years until she bought a house cash.

Next up: **"Not everything good fi eat good fi talk."** Translation? Just because something seems nice or tempting don't mean you should talk about it or even indulge in it. It is a cautionary reminder to keep certain things private, especially in a place where news travel faster than Wi-Fi.

Your auntie might share this one after reminding you not to tell the neighbors about her herbal remedies or her boyfriend, who is ten years her junior.

Keep yuh plans tight, yuh blessings quiet. Jamaicans value discretion. **"No mek yuh lef' hand know what yuh right hand a do"** is about moving wise. Not everything yuh building need announcement. Sometimes, silence is security.

When I was a girl, we had a neighbor who always had a story on her tongue. Morning, noon, and night, she would pass through the lane with news from every house. One day, she carried a tale about a quarrel that never happened, and before she knew it, the same people she gossiped about turned against her. Mi Madda shook her head and said, *"Cock mout kill cock."* From that day, I learned to keep some things in my heart, because as she reminded me, **"Wall have ears."**

"Mouth open, story jump out." Sometimes, yuh talk so much, yuh trip over truth yuh wasn't ready fi tell. Mi madda know when quiet was power. She seh: some tings better kept close 'til time ripe. If yuh always chatting, yuh give people reason fi ruin yuh. Learn fi guard yuh tongue and know when to speak and when to sip yuh tea.

"Silent riva run deep." Watch de quiet one. In Jamaica, silence often means depth. Some people nuh talk much, but dem thinking, watching, and waiting. Don't underestimate quiet people. Still waters run deep. Loud talk don't prove wisdom; steady action does. Growing up I learned to respect this elder in the community who hardly spoke, but when she did, everyone leaned in.

Don't assume silence mean surrender, or stillness mean stupidity. "A nuh every shut eye mean sleep" remind yuh that some people watching while pretending not to. Quiet nuh mean clueless. Jamaicans use these sayings fi warn yuh not to underestimate anyone. Some folks quiet because dem wise—dem listening, learning, and waiting fi di right time to move. "Don't tek man fi fool just because him quiet." Some people move silent because dem thinking deep, watch everything, and choose peace over performance. Jamaicans respect di one who nuh rush fi talk but always know what going on. Because when trouble come, it is often di quiet one who move swift and sure.

That's the deeper lesson here: quiet don't mean weak. It means measured, observant, and is often more powerful than blast. In a world full of noise, silence can be strategic.

So, mind yuh mouth. Because in this culture, speaking too quick often mean learning too late.Ms. Mills, my fifth-grade teacher loved to say: **"A see yuh cyan see, or a nah see yuh nah see,"** when we get the math problem wrong due to carelessness. What she meant was simple, seeing isn't just about eyesight but also common sense. It's about sense. People often ignore what's right in front of them, whether from denial, pride, or convenience. I use it when I send Winsome for the remote and it right on the table and she seh don't see it.

"A nuh who you see, a who see you." Sometimes you think you watching people but is dem watching you. Be mindful of how you move. Character show in the shadows same way it show in the spotlight. Somebody always taking note.

Then there's the spicy warning: **"Trouble mek monkey eat pepper."** It is a colorful way of saying, "Play stupid games, win spicy prizes." In other words, meddle in what doesn't concern you, and you'll feel the heat. Like that time mi cousin tink he could outtalk a police officer on the road and ended up walking home, barefoot.

Some people don't understand struggle until dem feel it. **"Rockstone a river bottom nuh know sun hot"** is how Jamaicans describe sheltered minds. When yuh cushioned from hardship, yuh talk reckless. This teach yuh fi be mindful, don't judge what yuh never live.

Jamaican trickster Anancy survive not because him strong, but because him smart. **"Anancy know which leaf fi hide under"** mean even clever people know where to duck and when to run. Wisdom sometimes look like hiding, not losing.

"Scornful dawg nyam dutty pudden." Never look down on people or things you think beneath you. Life have a funny way a turning tables: today you scorn it, tomorrow you need it. Pride will starve you, but humility will always feed you.

"Never look a gift horse in the mouth" is international, yes, but the Jamaican delivery adds a certain weight. If someone blesses you with something, take it with humility, even if it is not brand new, your favorite color, or quite your style. Complaining about free things is a fast track to being labeled "ungrateful", a title worse than "lazy" in Jamaican households.

Sometimes, di loudest person in di room have di least substance. **"Empty barrel mek di most noise"** call out boastfulness and big talk wid no backing. Jamaicans value

30

humility backed by action. True wisdom don't haffi holler, it show up in how yuh live.

"Stick bruk inna yuh eaz?" Mi madda used dis when di pickney dem stubborn till it hurt. It mean when warning fall pon deaf ears, if yuh nuh tek correction, consequence ago lick yuh same way. Wisdom nuh just in hearing: it in listening.

"Wanti wanti cyah getti, and getti getti nuh wanti." Now this one stings. It is the cruel irony of life: the ones who desperately want something can't seem to get it, while those who have it take it for granted. Like the young woman who change jobs like she change clothes, while Miss Mac up the street with five mouts fi feed cyan fine a job fi save her life. Jamaican proverbs cut deep like that.

"What eye don't see, heart don't leap." Sometimes ignorance protect peace. Mi madda seh, "Don't go looking fi trouble, sometimes is better fi nuh know." Not every truth build, some truths bruise. Wisdom is knowing what fi hold, what fi release, and what fi leave alone.

"Every day bucket go a well, one day di bottom will drop out." You might think you're getting away with cutting corners, but eventually, that strategy will fail. Whether it is lying on the job, cheating the system, or staying in a toxic pattern, this proverb is a warning: constant pressure will eventually lead to collapse. Check your bucket before it is too late.

Too much trouble round yuh? No wonder yuh cyah rest. **"Too much rat nah mek dog sleep,"** describe constant stress, distraction, and pressure. It is a warning to clear yuh space. Protect yuh peace. Even di big dog need calm fi watch di yard.

"Self-praise is no recommendation." Jamaicans believe respect come from others, not from blowing yuh own trumpet. Mi madda seh: "Let yuh work talk louder than yuh mouth." Bragging cheap; good character priceless.

"If ah did know, dog nyam yuh supper" is what yuh hear when regret come too late. Hindsight sweet, but it can't change the outcome. Jamaicans use this fi say: if yuh did listen, yuh wouldn't be inna di mess. Wisdom is knowing before, so pay attention early, before yuh chance gone.

On the subject of resources and responsibility, we hear the phrase **"Waste not, want not."** This is often said while scraping every last bit of condensed milk from the tin or buttering the bread- back to go with your tea. It is about stretching what you have and not living wastefully. The message is simple: what you discard today, you might be begging for tomorrow.

"What sweet yuh gwine sour yuh." Be cautious of short-term pleasures that have long-term consequences. That extra glass of milk might be delicious now but wait 'til your stomach start to "bubble like soup." Or ramp too much and someone gets hurt. It is a broader caution to think beyond the moment and to consider what comes after the thrill.

"The grass is not always greener on the other side." Sometimes, in pursuit of a fancier life, people abandon perfectly good things. Like James' uncle who left his decent job for a "big opportunity" in Cayman, only to return months later with less money and a bad cough. Jamaicans remind yuh, **"A bird in di hand betta than two inna bush."** Contentment is a gift. Don't give weh surety fi unsurity or otherwise, hold on to what sure, before yuh lose it chasing illusion.

"Respect your elders" makes another appearance here, not just as a matter of manners, but as a means of preserving wisdom and knowledge. Your elders have lived through hurricanes, heartbreaks, and hard times. Their stories aren't just nostalgia; they're instruction manuals with missing pages.

Frog seh, what is joke to you is death to me." Mi madda used dis to teach compassion. What small to yuh might be big to somebody else. Wisdom is weighing impact, not just intent.

"Not all that glitter is gold." That flashy job, that sweet-talking partner, that investment promising double returns in two weeks, if it sounds too good to be true, it probably is. Jamaican wisdom urges discernment. Because in a world full of shine, it is easy to mistake polish for value.

"Good friend better than pocket money." You can spend pocket money in a day, but a good friend will carry you through life. Mi madda always drop dis one when tings tight, like back-to-school time when shoe sole thin and school fee high. Because when pressure drop, money buy food, yes— but friend bring pot, spoon, and story fi cheer yuh up while yuh eat. Whether it is borrowing $500 'til payday or showing up wid soup when yuh sick, true friendship in Jamaica is currency. And trust me, it appreciates wid interest. When yuh cyah call Western Union, yuh is called Marcia. When yuh cyah carry di weight, is yuh bredren shoulder hold yuh. Money come and go, but a good friend? That one multiply joy and divide sorrow. **"Money mek fren, and money bruk fren."** In Jamaica, nothing tests relationships like cash. One minute you're close, the next you're enemies over a borrowed thousand dollars. This proverb reminds us that money can both attract and divide, so be cautious about who you trust, and never let money determine devotion.

"Don't lend more than you can afford to lose." Granny always warned, "If you cyah sleep without it, don't lend it." Lending money isn't just about generosity; it is about emotional readiness. If you can't part with it without resentment, keep it. Jamaican wisdom teaches that peace of mind is worth more than recompense.

"Look before you leap." This one could save lives, literally and figuratively. It is about slowing down, evaluating your next move, and asking, "Is this really a good idea?" before committing. Especially when that move involves taking a loan from a man named "Choppy or a job with a shady boss."

"Every hoe have him stick a bush." In other words, everyone has someone out there for them, no matter how strange, odd, or downright difficult they may seem. You might not see it now, but somebody out there thinks your uncle Trevor, with his socks-and-sandals fashion and obsession with dominoes and redstripe, is a catch.

"Not everything you want is good for you." Just because you crave it doesn't mean you need it or should have it. Whether it is a toxic relationship, a job that pays well but drains your soul, or a third helping of curry goat, restraint is wisdom.

And finally, **"Too many cooks spoil the broth."** This one speaks to chaos by committee. When too many hands meddle, confusion tek over. A task with too much chatter seldom finish right. Everybody giving orders and nobody doing the work. Unity need order, and success need focus. Everybody can't lead, somebody haffi steer.

These proverbs are survival tools. They teach us to move with intention, humility, and discernment. Each one, wrapped in humor and hard-earned truth, offers a glimpse into the collective wisdom of a people who have seen it all and still find a way to laugh, love, and live well.

Wisdom From Mi Madda

Chapter 4

Iron Sharpens Iron

Discipline in Jamaican culture is not about strict rules for the sake of control; it is about molding you into someone who can handle life with sense, strength, and pride. They don't glamorize failure, but they sure know how to teach from it. When you mess up, expect a lecture, not a pat on the back. From early on, children learn that growth isn't accidental; it is earned through effort, humility, and obedience. If you want good results, you'd better be willing to put in some hard work.

Let's start with one of the pillars of progress: **"Get yuh education."** In a Jamaican household, this isn't just advice; it is doctrine. Whether your goal is to become a doctor, an artist, or the best pastry chef in the country, education is often seen as the key to escaping struggle and achieving independence. Your mother may not have finished high school, but she'll make sure you reach university, even if it means selling puddings on Sundays. "Nobody cyan tek knowledge from yuh," she'll say, and she means it.

Success have a timeline, and it start now. **"Plant yuh corn early if yuh waan reap early"** remind yuh that dreams need discipline. Jamaicans know: if yuh want results next year, start sowing today. Nuh wait fi di perfect moment, start wid what yuh have.

"Live clean, let yuh work be seen" is more than a lifestyle, it is a philosophy. It teach yuh to move with integrity, knowing that consistency speak louder than performance. In Jamaica, greatness is seen in how yuh carry yuhself, not how loud yuh brag.

Right beside that comes the equally serious command: **"Work hard for what you want."** Nothing is more shameful than laziness unless its laziness paired with entitlement. You want new shoes? Go help yuh uncle with his construction work. You want a phone? Go sell bag juice after school.

"Mek hay while di sunshine" mean use your opportunity while yuh have it. Life nuh wait. In Jamaican homes, this is how yuh get reminded that idleness waste potential. Whether it is time, youth, or resources, seize it before it gone. Life owes you nothing but the opportunity to try. And if you slack off, don't worry, someone will remind you. Gladly.

Now, a particularly sharp warning: **"Don't licky licky."** It is not about appetite; it is about integrity. A "licky licky" person accepts anything from anyone, without standards or self-respect. That's the type of person who gets in trouble because they couldn't say "no" to free things. In short: don't sell your soul for a snack. Your mother will tell you straight: "if yuh belly control yuh, yuh always inna mix-up."

"Hard ears pickney dead a sun hot" warn yuh that disobedience come with real consequences. Parents nuh just talk fi talk sake. If dem say, "Don't go outside," and yuh go anyway, yuh might find out why the hard way. Wisdom begin with listening,

Learning hard lesson once is enough. **"No mek di same stick lick yuh two time"** is a Jamaican warning against repeating mistakes. If you slip once, tighten yuh step. Don't wait for the same mistake to embarrass yuh twice. Yuh don't need to fail three times to know something nuh work. Wise people learn fast, wiser ones learn from others.

"Mi fren bring mi come, but mi cyah bring mi fren back." Translation? Your friend may open the door, but how you act determines if you get to stay. This proverb highlights individual responsibility even in communal spaces. Jamaicans teach early: you represent more than yourself, and one bad attitude can close doors for many.

"Every hoe haffi sit down pon dem own stick" is Jreminder that yuh reputation, effort, and choices follow yuh, regardless of who helped yuh get there. This one mean: accountability cyah be shared. Everybody mus' bear di weight of dem own actions.

Discipline is also about knowing your place, especially as a child. That's where **"say good morning to everyone who cross you path"** comes back with new meaning. It is not just manners; it is mental training. A child who learns to greet others with respect becomes an adult who knows how to conduct themselves with dignity in any room. Walk into a gathering and say nothing? That's an insult. Walk in and say "Mawnin'," even to strangers? That's pure class.

"Mi likkle but mi tallawah." Size don't measure strength. Many people small in body but big in courage and spirit. Character is not about what people see, but the backbone inside you. Mi madda would laugh when people underestimate her small frame, then humble them wid action. This proverb raise generations fi know that stature nuh determine strength. Walk humble, yes, but walk tall.

This one spicy. **"Mi throw mi corn, mi nuh call no fowl"** is how Jamaicans drop truth without naming names. It mean if yuh guilty, yuh will feel it. It is also a masterclass in accountability: when truth drop, yuh spirit will know if it fit.

"First time is a mistake; second time is purpose." Now this one hits different. It is not just about learning from errors; it is about taking responsibility. Repeat a bad choice, and you've turned foolishness into habit, and that's when consequences land like coconuts. If you keep touching the iron and getting burned, don't expect sympathy. Expect aloe vera and a lecture.

"Who cyan hear will feel." This one is almost a threat, but a gentle, loving one. It is the Caribbean version of "Hard head make soft behind." If you don't listen to wisdom, you'll end up learning the hard way.

I will never forget the time I skipped homework for two days straight. First day, mi teacher gave mi a warning. Second day, she gave mi a lashing in front of the class. Mi Madda didn't even defend me, she only said, *"Who cyah hear, mus' feel."* The first warning was mercy. The second, a lesson. That beating taught me more discipline than any lecture could, and it's why I never went to school unprepared again.

40

"Shortcut draw blood." Here's where one of the most sobering proverbs comes in: This isn't just about choosing the longer path; it is about respecting the process. When you rush success or try to cheat your way through life, you often end up hurting yourself. Like the student who copied another's homework, only to get caught and suspended. Or the young man who borrowed money from a "quick loan" man and ended up paying double, with interest and fear. There are no shortcuts worth bleeding for.

And when all the encouragement has been offered, when books are bought, uniforms pressed, and every motivational speech delivered, there's still the hard truth: **"You can carry horse to water, but you cyah force it to drink."** You can provide every opportunity, but people mus' choose to grow. Yuh parents can wake you at 5 a.m., pack your lunch, and send you to school, but if you sleep in class? That's on you. Love will provide the way, but you have to walk it.

Still, old habits die hard, and sometimes, they return sweeter than they left. That's why you'll hear, **"Old fire stick easy fi ketch."** Whether it is an ex, an old bad habit, or a former lifestyle, familiar things are easy to reignite. It is a warning to stay vigilant with your boundaries. What you thought was burned out might still be smoldering and waiting for a breeze.

"If yuh want good, yuh nose haffi run." In other words, success demands sacrifice. You might cry, sweat, or stumble, but press on. Jamaicans don't hand out sympathy for shortcuts but celebrate those who push through.

In My Madda households, discipline is a mix of guidance and grim humor. It is the blend of love, lecture, and a little tough love that teaches you to stand firm, speak clearly, and earn your way. You'll grow up understanding that ambition without discipline is like soup without salt; it might fill you, but it won't satisfy.

"Show me yuh company and mi tell yuh who yuh be." Mi madda never miss a beat wid dis one, because your circle shape yuh. Sit with five slack people, and chances are, yuh become the sixth.

Or as she'd say with a grin: **"Pigeon nuh keep party wid parrot."** In other words, birds of a feather flock together, but inna Jamaica, even birds have sense. Who yuh walk wid say plenty 'bout where yuh going. Stay close to people who sharpen yuh edge, not dull yuh shine.

"Yuh cyah plant corn and reap peas." You can't fake effort and expect excellence. Every action yields fruit according to its seed. If you're sowing carelessness, expect consequences. Jamaican life is full of trials, but also full of choice.

Same sun, different outcome. **"Same sun weh melt di wax, harden di clay"** remind yuh that how life shape yuh depend on what yuh made of. Some people break under pressure, others get stronger.

So, work hard, stay humble, and don't let your ambitions outgrow your abilities. Because in this culture, discipline isn't punishment, it is preparation for life. Iron sharpen iron, but yuh character determine di edge.

Anette Rose White

Chapter 5

Character and Connection

Let's begin with a simple truth wrapped in a sing-song threat: **"Play wid puppy, puppy lick yuh mouth."** It is a cheeky way of saying, "Know your boundaries." If you get too familiar, you might end up in a situation you're not prepared for. One minute you're joking with your boss, the next minute you're being written up for disrespect. In other words: familiarity breeds contempt, especially if you're not ready for the mess you helped stir up.

Then there's the hotter version: **"Play wid fire, you will get burn."** Self-explanatory, but it hits different when delivered in your mother's tone as you head out in clothes she deems "too tight" for decent company. The idea is simple: certain risks are not worth the fallout. Whether it is a dangerous relationship, shady job, or illegal hustle, fire might start off warm, but it will scorch you in the end.

Playfulness has limits. What begins as small mischief can grow into real trouble if we don't draw the line. That is why even laughter needs wisdom to guide it.

"Is not who you see, is who see you." Now this one is pure paranoia and pure genius. Just because you're not watching doesn't mean you're not being watched. Jamaicans live with a built-in surveillance system: neighbors, vendors, old ladies with sharp vision and sharper tongues. Before you even think of acting out, remember somebody is always seeing, even if yuh nuh see dem. So, mind yuh manners, fix yuh clothes, and don't embarrass your family name.

"Wall have ears." This remind us to be cautious because someone is always watching, listening, or remembering. Gossip travels faster than taxis in rush hour, and what you say in passing can land in places you never intended. As Granny might whisper while casting a look toward the neighbor's window, "Talk low, wall have ears, enuh." The art of discretion is survival, whether in the market, at school, or even in the home.

And when words become dangerous, silence becomes wisdom. That's where another powerful pair of proverbs steps in: **"See and blind, hear and deaf."** Observe but don't always respond. Hear what's said but know when to stay quiet. This isn't about ignorance; it is about self-preservation. Whether in family drama, workplace politics, or street-side debates, knowing when to play blind or deaf can help you maintain your dignity and your business integrity. As Jamaicans know well, not every fight is yours, and not every truth needs to be told aloud.

Life nuh easy right now. **"Dis ya time too rough fi mek fool"** is how Jamaicans warn yuh: use yuh head. Resources scarce, trust low, and stakes high, this is not di season fi play careless. The world watching, bills piling, and opportunity short, so sharpen yuh wits and guard yuh choices.

"Don't cut your nose to spite your face." When anger blind yuh, sometimes you hurt yourself more than the person you vex wid. Pride can mek you throw away blessing just to prove a point. Wisdom is learning when to let go, when to step back, and when peace worth more than being right.

"Same dawg bite you a morning bite you a evening." Beware of those who have already revealed themselves to you. If someone has betrayed your trust or disrespected you once, don't be shocked when it happens again. As Granny might say, *"Fool me once, shame on you. Fool me twiceshame on me."* This proverb reminds us to learn quickly and protect our peace.

Acting like yuh don't know can sometimes backfire. **"If yuh play fool, yuh mus' get fool"** remind yuh that pretending ignorance too long might make people treat yuh like yuh really slow. Play smart, not stupid, because in trying to blend in, yuh might end up in di mix-up yuh were trying to dodge.

Of course, not everyone who smile wid yuh mean yuh well. **"Every smile nuh mean teeth clean."** Some people laugh wid yuh but carry envy deep. Wisdom teach watch action, not only words.

"Same knife stick sheep stick goat." Don't assume betrayal can't come from those close to yuh. Sometimes the one who share yuh table is the one who test yuh strength.

"Sorry fi mawga dawg him tun round bite yuh."
Sometimes, your sympathy backfire. You feel bad for
somebody, take them in, and next thing you know, dem
eating your food, borrowing yuh clothes, and chatting yuh
behind yuh back. This proverb is a nice way to say, "Help
people, yes, but don't be foolish." There's a fine line between
kind and naïve, and Jamaicans are experts at pointing it out.

And if that bite turn into you biting somebody else? Don't
be surprised. **"Ef yuh cyah ketch Quakoo, yuh ketch him
shut."** When people cyah get back at the real cause of dem
pain, dem lash out at whoever nearby. It is a caution against
misdirected anger. Be mindful, hurting someone else won't
heal your wound, and blaming dem won't fix the problem.

"The higher monkey climb, the more him expose." Ah,
yes, the perfect proverb for the overly ambitious. Without
humility, as people rise in life, dem flaws become more
visible. Want a promotion? Want fame? Better make sure
yuh foundation strong because higher visibility means more
scrutiny. As your grandmother might say, "Don't go showing
off when yuh stitch dem crooked."

Mi madda would shake her head and say, **'Neva see, come
see'**. Some people, when dem first meet good fortune,
behave boasy and careless, like dem never see blessing yet.
Character is tested not just in hardship, but in how yuh
hangle plenty. A humble spirit don't need to show off
because true worth keep quiet. New status shouldn't erase
old manners. Humility never go out of style."

"Cockroach nuh business inna fowl fight." This is one of
those sayings that slaps you with its accuracy. It means don't

insert yourself into conflicts that have nothing to do with you, especially if you're the weaker party. Like jumping into your coworkers' argument only to end up the one written up or meddling in office drama and getting cursed from both sides. Some things are above your pay grade. Walk away.

"Deaf ears man give news carrier trouble." Pretending you didn't hear something don't stop consequences from happening. If someone give yuh a warning and you ignore it? That's your problem. Jamaicans don't tolerate willful ignorance. Your uncle warned you not to park under the mango tree. Now you're out there cleaning sap off your windshield with a face like boiled dumpling.

"Chicken merry, hawk deh near." Just when you start to feel relaxed, life reminds you that danger can be right around the corner. That sweet moment of calm before the storm? Classic hawk behavior. This proverb is often whispered during celebrations or play, reminding folks not to get too comfortable. Like when Trevor buy a flashy car pon loan, even though him workplace already talking 'bout layoffs "Chicken merry," Granny says, "but hawk watching."

"When man inna trouble, pickney clothes fit him" When hardship knock, pride nuh get to answer di door. Trouble level everybody. It strip title, ego, and false image 'til yuh realize comfort matter more than status. In times of real trouble, yuh make do with whatever is available, even if it's not ideal.

"Trouble mek monkey eat pepper." Dis one? Mi madda laughed when she seh it, but di truth behind it sting. Because when yuh back against di wall, even di most unlikely choice suddenly become necessary. Di same man who swear him would "never" now walking the path him use to scorn, just to save him skin.

Jamaicans know trouble don't knock. It just push door and step right in. And when it does, yuh better learn fi bend, adapt, and humble yuhself quick. Joy often walks with danger close behind. The wise heart celebrate, yes, but also prepare because trouble never announce itself.

Together, these sayings remind yuh: don't be quick to judge who doing what, or why. Until yuh in dem shoes, or barefoot in dem struggle, yuh don't know what desperation require. So, mind yuh mouth, soften yuh eye, and always, always walk wid a little grace in yuh spirit. Because one day it could be you.

"Sickness is no respecter of person." Mi madda use to say, "Sickness nuh ask fi résumé, it just show up and sit down." Whether yuh a CEO or a cane cutter, once sickness enter, we all lay flat same way. It is a sobering reminder that flesh is flesh, and health is not a guarantee, no matter how strong, young, or important yuh think yuh be.

This proverb teach respect and humility. Check how yuh treat people, because one day yuh might need dem same hands to hold yuh up. It also teach compassion, when yuh see somebody battling sickness or hardship, don't act like it is a passing shadow. Yuh just nuh reach deh yet. Life can turn in a second.

So, hold yuh judgment, lift yuh gratitude, and take care of yuh body, but more so, yuh heart. Because sickness, like rain, fall pon everybody roof.

"When banana wan dead it shoot." Sometimes, signs of change or endings appear just before a breakthrough or breakdown. Like a relationship suddenly filled with sweet gestures before a breakup. Or a company giving bonuses before laying off staff. This proverb urges you to read the signs and prepare your spirit: the bloom before the wither is no coincidence.

"New broom sweep clean, but old broom know di corner." Mi madda use to grin when she seh dis, especially when di young and shiny show up acting like dem invented sweepin'. New broom full of energy, yes. It sweep fast, loud, and wid confidence. But ask it to find di stubborn dirt 'round back? Ask it how to reach under di cabinet without scattering everything else? That's when yuh realize Energy cyah replace experience.

Old broom might look worn, but it know where di mess hide. It bend in di right places, move quiet, and get di job done without performance. Inna workplace, life, or family, this proverb remind yuh: don't overlook di wisdom of experience just because it nuh wear gloss.

So, when di intern full of ideas or di new manager walked in wid PowerPoint and pride, tek note, but also tek time fi ask Ms. Patsy from payroll how things *really* run. Because new might shine, but old still know where di cobwebs hide.

Value freshness, yes, but don't throw 'way di broom dat know di house.

"Fire deh a muss-muss tail, him tink a cool breeze." This one is comedy and warning rolled in one. The possum (muss-muss) feels the heat on its tail but thinks it is just wind. It is the Jamaican way of saying: if something feels off, it probably *is*. Don't ignore the signs; otherwise, you'll regret it. Whether it is your partner acting shady or your car making a strange sound, trust the signs, not your wishful thinking.

"Trouble nuh set like rain." Rain give yuh warning, cloud roll in, breeze pick up, the skys get heavy. But trouble don't. It just start. No thunder. No cloud. Just boom - yuh in a mess. This proverb call yuh to stay grounded, prepared, and prayerful. Because life move fast and not always in yuh favor.

Be vigilant. You check yuh tire before a long drive, you save a likkle from each pay, keep one eye open. Not because you expect trouble, but because you respect how life can shift without knocking.

And when trouble come, this saying soften the shock. It says: **You didn't miss the signs; there weren't any. So don't beat up yuhself**. Just hold firm, lean on faith, and remember, trouble don't last always, but it surely don't send invitation either.

"Sometimes coffee, sometimes tea." Life isn't always going to serve what you ordered. Some days you get exactly what you want. Other days, you're forced to take what's available. This proverb is about resilience, knowing how to accept life's ups and downs without losing control. Today it is steak, tomorrow it is sardines. Humble yourself.

Some people see yuh calm and think yuh clueless. **"Yuh cyah see mi an' tek mi fi fool"** is Jamaica's way of warning: don't mistake meekness for weakness. Many a wise person keep dem mouth shut until di moment call fi action. So, mind who yuh underestimating, silence nuh mean senseless.

These proverbs round out a cultural toolkit filled with humor, depth, and timeless wisdom. They are playful but piercing. They teach through laughter, warn through metaphor, and leave you better prepared for life's surprises. In Jamaica, wit isn't just entertainment; it is education. And if you've made it this far, you've been well-schooled.

Anette Rose White

Chapter Six

Fate, Effort, and Consequence

Yuh see dis life? It full a twists and turns. Sometimes yuh run fast and still buck yuh toe. Other time, blessings just fall like rain. But no matter how it come, sweet or sour, be wise. Because fate nuh always fair, and effort nuh always pay same time. But yuh see consequence? Consequence always clock in.

Life don't always deliver blessings in the moment we expect. What belongs to you will find its way, but only if you have the patience to wait and the strength to keep walking. Like mi madda say, **"What is fi yuh cyah be un-fi yuh."** Because when life slow down and doors close, dis saying hold yuh true. What is written fi yuh cyah miss yuh, not by delay, not by detour, not even by sabotage. What's yours will still be yours, but yuh haffi stay ready fi receive it. Just because yuh time nuh come yet nuh mean it nah come, sometimes, yuh just haffi have faith and keep walking steady.

"What nuh kill, fatten." Hardship rough when yuh in it, but it strengthen you in ways you never see until later. The trials you survive become the very thing that shape your backbone. Trouble might hurt you, but it also teach resilience. So, hush chile, fi yuh time soon come.

"Who laugh last, laugh best." Let di chapter finish before yuh clap or cry. Mi madda say this wid a smirk when people gloat too early. Life nuh done 'til it done.

"Don't be fool-fool now. Trouble teach better than teacher." Mi madda used to clap her hands together after saying this one, like punctuation. Because while teacher come wid blackboard and bell, trouble come wid consequence and cost. Life nuh waste chalk, it mark yuh wid experience. Some lessons yuh skip inna school, life go mek sure yuh repeat dem in real time. And trust mi, life nuh grade pon curve. So, if yuh keep running headfirst into di same wall, don't blame fate, blame stubbornness. Wisdom not always sweet, but it sure effective when pain mark yuh notebook.

"Willful wastes bring woeful wants." Careless hands soon find empty pockets. When yuh treat what yuh have with respect, it multiply; when yuh careless with it, poverty come knocking quick. Waste is a seed that grow into regret. Be wise with resources, for today's feast can turn into tomorrow's famine.

"Yuh spread yuh bed, yuh haffi lay dung inna it." Life is about choices, and every choice has consequence. Once you mek yuh choice, good or bad, you must live wid it. It's a call to responsibility; don't blame others for the path you pave yourself.

"What gone bad a morning cyah come good evening."
From early morning yuh smell di pot bun up, but instead of turning off di stove, yuh stir it harder and add seasoning. Mi madda seh: once something start spoil, don't pretend it can fix itself. Whether relationship, business deal, or moral compromise, some things rotten too deep fi revive. It nuh mean yuh heartless fi walk 'way; it mean yuh wise enough to stop feeding barren soil. Not every situation deserve redemption.

"Yuh cyah cross di same river twice." Mi madda seh this like scripture. Di river might look familiar, but it is di current dat shift. Life move. People change. Even yuh reflection inna dat water different from di last time. So don't enter every situation with old mindset. Yesterday's tools cyah solve today's problem. If yuh approach di new season wid old sense, prepare fi drown in assumptions.

"Pick a lane, stand firm." Half-foot don't build house. Commitment is where character start. Whether it is a job, relationship, or principle, choose your side and root deep. People who float like leaf never grow like tree.

"Tek what you get til yuh get weh yuh want." Patience is not weakness; it is strategy. Sometimes yuh haffi accept small beginnings while yuh work toward bigger dreams. Resilience doesn't mean settling, it means holding your head high while you press forward. That temporary job. That cramped apartment. Take it.

That's why mi madda always say, **"Yuh cyah serve two masters.***"* Pleasing everybody is a sure way to losing yuhself. If yuh always shifting to suit people, yuh soul start split in pieces. Loyalty mus' have direction. Follow purpose, not applause.

And hear this: **"Yuh cyah both ride horse and hold cow."** Ambition is good. But scattered focus bring frustration. Every season demand priority. Decide who yuh helping, what yuh building, and where yuh heading, then drop di rest. You cyah gallop and tug at di same time. Choose one and commit strong.

"Everybody want sweet life, but who willing fi sweat fi it?" Mi madda never glamorized hard life, but she respected it. She'd say: "Everybody love blessing, but not everybody love process." And di truth is, sugar don't come before chopping cane. Everybody post dem victory online, but very few show dem 5 a.m. hustle, di tears behind closed door, or di nights yuh go sleep wid empty belly and full dream. Success cost something. Be willing to pay in full.

"Yuh cyah fatten cow pon market day." Last-minute effort cyah fix a lifetime of neglect. Mi madda beat dis into our heads: preparation is love made visible. Yuh cyah wait til exam day fi study or wedding day fi learn loyalty. Some things haffi build long before spotlight. If yuh wait til curtain rise to practice, yuh nuh serious 'bout di stage.

"No wait till yuh thirsty fi dig well." Wisdom builds before crisis. Mi madda store rice and truth same way, in reserve. She seh: "Don't wait 'til yuh need help fi create support. Sow in peace what yuh want in trouble." Whether it is skill, savings, or strength, start now. Preparedness nuh just smart, it honorable.

"Better to bend than to break." Mi madda seh: "Stiff-neck people break easy." Pride full up yuh chest, but humility protect yuh back. Sometimes, survival mean adapting. Not giving up, just shifting weight so yuh don't crack under pressure. Bending nuh mean weak, it mean resourceful. Because breeze come fi everybody. But di ones who bend? Dem still standing.

"Nuh put yuh basket weh yuh cyah reach it." Ambition is beautiful, but it mus' wear boots, not wings. Mi madda didn't stop we from dreaming, she just made sure di dreams come wid plan. Dream big, yes, but build step by step. If yuh set goals too far fi touch, disappointment replace discipline. Reach up, yes, but know how to climb.

"So yuh see, chile? Life nuh simple. But di wisdom from long time still guide we step. Walk good. Think clear. And when di wind change, stand firm or sway smart. Either way, move wid sense."

Because in this life, it nuh matter how rough di road, what matter is how yuh walk it.

Chapter 7

Character, Connection, and Clarity

E very word carry weight. And once it drop, yuh cyah tek it back. **"Think before yuh talk."** Mi madda seh dis with her eyes more than her mouth. Character start long before action, it show up in how yuh speak, how yuh treat people, and how yuh stand when pressure come.

"Chile, character carry yuh further than charm. Discernment save yuh from mix-up. But above all, connection a gold. Is not money build life, is people."

Mi madda nuh waste time wid pretense. She teach we early: shiny outside cyah fix rotten inside. Charm might get yuh in di door, but only character keep yuh welcome. And connection? That's di rope yuh hold when life tek turn and yuh hand slippery. A well-lived life nuh build off applause, it build off people who show up when everybody else disappear.

"Time longer than rope." Patience is power. You may not see justice today but trust me: wrongdoers eventually trip over their own lies. This proverb is a comfort to the quiet ones, the overlooked, the bypassed, who know that what's delayed is not denied. Rope might fray and snap, but time, time outlast all things. Don't rush what God preparing. Hold yuh posture. Hold di faith.

"Good friend come from hard times." Yuh want to know who real? Watch who stay when yuh nuh have nutten fi offer. Storm reveal substance. Mi madda seh: easy season full up wid crowd, but when di cupboard bare and yuh spirit low, is only the true friends stick 'round. Some people smile bright when yuh high but turn ghost when yuh fall. But di one who walk wid yuh through rain and shame, dem yuh keep close, bless daily, and never tek fi granted.

"Backra massa days done." Don't wait for permission fi shine. Di days of servitude done; yuh born fi lead, not follow blindly. Don't shrink yuhself just to mek others comfortable. Walk tall, talk straight, and build wid pride. Freedom not just law, it is posture, mindset, and how yuh answer to yuh own name.

Mi madda cook truth same way she cook soup, slow, seasoned, and plenty simmer. She'd stop stirring, look me dead in di eye and say: **"No open yuh mouth without yuh brain."** Because careless words travel faster than apology. One wrong sentence mash up friendship, ruin opportunity, or stir up war yuh cyah undo. Talking is easy. Thinking take discipline. And silence? Sometimes, that's wisdom in disguise.

Move By Principle, Not Performance because "Ants follow fat, not promise." Mi madda teach we: people nuh follow hype, they follow results. Don't get caught up in who chat loudest or shine brightest. Follow fruit, not flash. Is not di man wid di mic yuh watch, it is di one wid track record. Promise might sound sweet, but production taste sweeter.

"Mi chile, clarity is not just vision, it is intention. Character is not just how yuh walk, it is how yuh treat people when nobody looking. And connection? That's di bridge yuh walk on in storm. Build it strong. Speak it true. And let yuh life clap louder than yuh mouth.

In Jamaica relationships are built on discipline. Family, friends, neighbors, everybody play a role in shaping who yuh become. And just like iron sharpening iron, sometimes sparks fly before the edge get fine.

"One han' cyah clap." Try it. Clap wid one hand and yuh get breeze, not sound. Life works same way. Success is a group project, even when yuh name on di paper. No matter how independent yuh think yuh are, there's always a moment when yuh need somebody else.

Whether it is raising pickney, building business, or surviving a hard season, yuh need community. Mi madda never shame to ask for help nor too proud to offer it. She seh: "Independence sweet, but interdependence strong." Teamwork build legacy.

"If yuh cyaan dance a yard, yuh cyaan dance abroad." Charity, manners, and respect start at home. If you don't practice discipline in your own yard, don't expect the world to train yuh. Mi madda was fierce about this: she seh the world too rough to teach you basics. Home is rehearsal for destiny.

That's why Jamaicans say, **"No call di piper till di dance done."** In other words, don't celebrate too soon. Mi madda warn: some people hype up halfway, then flop. Don't start celebration when page one sweet. Wait 'til di chapter end. She'd warn: "Victory nuh confirmed by drumroll, but by endurance." Let di dust settle before yuh declare champion

At the same time, life not fair for everybody. **"Puss and dawg nuh have di same luck."** Some get chance easy, some fight fi every little step. Mi madda used dis to teach us not to measure our journey against others. Stay in yuh lane. What open for one might be closed fi yuh, but yuh still can reach if yuh patient and persistent.

Years later, when I moved abroad, I carried Mi Madda's wisdom in my pocket like lunch money. I saw a woman, she tried to bargain with the shopkeeper the same way we do back home. She was laughed at, embarrassed, and she left empty-handed. Mi Madda's words echoed in my mind: *"If yuh cyaan dance a yard, yuh cyaan dance abroad."* It wasn't that her way was wrong, but she hadn't learned the new steps yet. And yet, the old market women who had been there longer moved with confidence, they knew every corner, proving, as the proverb says, *"New broom sweep clean, but old broom know di corner."*

Sometimes, the balance of power shift sudden. **"Big tree fall down, goat bite leaf"** show how di mighty can fall, and how people once afraid of yuh might turn bold when yuh down. Dis proverb remind yuh fi walk with grace at di top, because people watching, and di same folks yuh overlook might rise when yuh drop.

"Every dog have him day, and every puss him four o'clock." A vivid reminder of long-term consequences: In other words, everything and everyone has their appointed time. Today might not be yours but tomorrow might be. No matter how low yuh feel, life always circle back to give yuh chance. Wisdom seh: patience nuh kill, it prepare.

"Jackass seh di worl' nuh level." Some people always bawl that life unfair. And truth be told, life nuh fair. But mi madda would add: "Him back prove it." Hardship show up in everybody's story. The point is not fairness, but resilience. Stand tall, even when di load uneven.

But it's not all warning and hardship. Jamaicans also know how fi turn struggle into strength. **"Tek yuh hand and tun fashion."** This mean create something out of nothing. Innovation born out of lack. Yuh dress up poor meal with pepper sauce, yuh patch torn jeans until dem stylish. It's a reminder: resourcefulness beat riches.

"Stone inna mango tree mean mango ripe." People don't trouble dry bush. If yuh getting attention, good or bad, it might be because yuh doing something worthwhile. Jealousy, gossip, even sabotage? Sometimes it is confirmation yuh fruit coming in. Mi madda seh: don't get distracted by di noise, stay rooted and keep bearing fruit.

"A coward man keep sound bone." Bravery nuh always mean rushing into fight. Sometimes the wisest man is the one who walk away and live to see anoda day. Appeal don't prove itself in foolish risk, but in knowing when to stand and when to step aside.

At the end of the day, Jamaicans know truth: **"One hand wash the other, and both wash the face."** Life sweeter when people support each other. Struggles easier, blessings brighter, and even hardship bearable when yuh nuh carry it alone.

Just as character, connection, and clarity shape how we stand in the world, Mi madda remind us that wisdom is not only about who we are, but what we do. Choices carry weight, but timing, patience, and preparation decide whether those choices bring peace or pain.

She seh, "Character guide yuh step, but prudence, patience, and readiness keep yuh from stumble." And so, we turn now to wisdom in action, the foresight to plan, the restraint to wait, and the discipline to prepare before the storm come.

Chapter 8

Prudence and Patience

Mi madda always seh, "Prudence save yuh pocket, patience save yuh skin, and preparation save yuh soul." Life nuh require only strength, it call for sense, timing, and foresight. Many people stumble because dem a rush, talk too fast, or jump inna situation widout plan. True wisdom in action is learning when fi hush, when fi wait, and when fi prepare for the storm.

"Finga neva seh look here, him seh look deh." Wisdom nuh shout nor boast, it point quiet. Just like yuh finger guide yuh eye, discernment guide yuh life. She taught that discernment lives in silence, in noticing the small signs others miss, a subtle hint, or di silence after a quarrel. She would nod and whisper, *"Watch wid yuh spirit, not just yuh ear."* those who watch careful save themselves grief.

"If you han inna debil mout, tek time draw it out." Hurry cyaan mend trouble. Recklessness only deepen it. Madda say patience can save yuh, even if people call yuh coward. **"Coward man keep sound bone."** Better fi walk away today and live fi try again tomorrow. She adds, **"Patient man ride donkey."** Slow steps still reach market, while those who hurry often tumble by the roadside.

"Nuh wait til drum beat to grine yuh axe." Preparation nuh start when battle already ring out. Mi madda always sharpen knife, patch clothes, and save likkle change, likkle food "just in case." At di time, mi grumble, but later, when storm mash-up di shop and food scarce, dat likkle store of flour and rice mek we eat. Preparation is quiet armor, you only see its value when danger knock.

"Pound a fret cyan pay ounce a debt." Worry rob yuh strength but give yuh nothing in return." Worry neva pay one bill. Action and faith do. "Cry nuh pay di bursar." Mi madda would tease when she ketch mi bawling over school fee. Instead, she teach me to work odd jobs, save mi money, and pray. Fretting only take away today's strength. Action bring tomorrow's change.

I remember when mi bredda school fee was due, and him sit crying at di table, bawling that him would never get through, that the bursar would shame him before everyone. Madda seh, *"Pound a fret cyaan pay ounce a debt. Tears nuh pay bursar."* She pressed a wet cloth in him hand, fi clean him face, and sent him outside to do odd jobs for neighbors, sweeping yard, carrying water, running errands. Little by little, di money gather, and by term's start, the fee was paid.

Her lesson long lasting, fretting drain tomorrow's hope, but steady work build tomorrow's change.

"Nuh buy puss inna bag." Mi madda always warn, "Test before yuh trust." She seh appearances cyan fool, and what look shiny may hide trouble. I remember when mi bredda bought a bicycle cheap from a stranger. It look good in di moment, but two days later di chain snap and the wheel wobble like old cart. Madda laugh and say, *"See it deh? Yuh buy puss inna bag. If yuh nuh check first, yuh end up wid cat when yuh did think yuh buy rabbit."* Lesson? Look beneath the surface, ask questions, and don't jump quick at what seems too good to be true.

"Shoes alone know if stocking have hole." Mi madda always remind us that not every struggle show outside. A man may smile broad, dress neat, and still carry quiet pain under the surface. Just like only the shoe can feel the hole in the stocking, only the heart know the weight it bear. I remember one teacher at school who never miss class, always cheerful in front of us. Years later we learn she was walking home each night because she couldn't afford bus fare. Mi madda would shake her head and say, *"Shoes alone know if stocking have hole, so walk gentle wid people. Yuh never know weh dem carrying."*

"Humble calf suck di most milk." Quiet humility draw more blessing than pride ever could. Di calf that bawl loud often get push way, but di one dat bend head low get fed first. Madda seh, "Pride belly empty; humble belly full."

"Small axe chop big tree." Persistence tear down even giant problem. Mi uncle chop one mango tree whole summer, swing, sweat, rest, repeat. People laughed at him, but eventually, tree fell. Same way small, steady effort, study each night, save each week, bring big reward.

"If yuh nuh done climb hill, nuh dash weh yuh stick."
Keep your support until journey end. Mi madda always seh,
"Finish yuh journey before yuh fling 'way yuh help." I
remember one schoolmate who borrowed notes from a
friend all term. As soon as exam week start, him boasts and
say he don't need them again and hand them back. But the
night before the final paper, him realized plenty topics he
neva study yet. He scramble, beg, and fret, but it was too
late. Madda would say, *"See it deh? Yuh still on di hill, but
yuh dash weh yuh stick."*

The truth is that pride make us feel like we done when we
only halfway. Whether it's mentors, tools, or discipline,
hold on until yuh truly reach di top. Help is not a crutch is
what steady yuh climb.

**"Monkey mus know weh him gwine put him tail before
im order troussers."** it remind us that planning come
before presentation. She seh, *"Nuh rush to dress up di
outside if yuh nuh ready fi handle di inside."*

Like Calvin who get call for job interview. Him bought
brand-new suit, shiny shoes, and trim hair neat. But when
di manager start asking questions, him stumble, 'im neva
even prepare one answer. Afterward, he walked home
looking sharp but feeling shame. Madda chuckle and say,
*"Monkey muss know weh him gwine put him tail before him
order troussers. Clothes cyaan cover unprepared mind."*

Her lesson stay with me: don't rush to appear ready when
yuh nuh ready. Before yuh step out bold, make sure
foundation set. Planning before presentation save
embarrassment and build true success.

"Nuh count yuh chicken before dem hatch." Hope sweet, but it cyaan take it to di bank. Madda warned me "nuh spend money mi nuh yet earn". Opportunity cyan slip, egg cyan spoil. Wait fi reality before yuh rejoice.

And still, even when blessing already inna yuh hand, some people quick fi reach past it, chasing after what might come. That's when mi madda remind us:

"A bird in the hand is worth two in di bush." Gratitude keep yuh grounded. Mi madda always remind us to value what we have, instead of chasing shadows. She tell of one young man in di village who had a steady job at the post office. It neva make him rich, but it pay him every Friday without fail. When a fast-talking friend promise him "quick money" from a scheme, he quit the job and put all his savings in. Within months, the scheme collapsed and him left with nothing, no work, no savings. Better to hold firm to a sure blessing than gamble for promises that vanish.

Endurance build character. **"Suck salt outta wooden spoon."** Poverty lick we hard sometimes, yet we mek do wid what we have. Mi madda always stir pot wid old spoon, and laugh: "Salt taste same, whether spoon silver or wood." She show that endurance build character.

"Too much a one ting good fi nutten." Mi madda always seh balance sweet, but excess spoil di taste. Life was never meant fi live lopsided. Too much sugar turn tea sickly, too much sleep breed laziness, too much work mash up body same way. She would laugh and remind us, *"Even rain, if it fall too long, flood di yard."*

Her point was clear, moderation is di key. In food, in work, in love, even in ambition, balance is what keep di soul steady.

"Two head betta dan one." Collaboration bring sense, even from unexpected place. Don't trust yuh own thinking alone, another mind might save yuh. Even if di other person nuh have all di wisdom, two head put together see further than one eye.

I remember when di roof start leak heavy one rainy season. Mi uncle wanted to fix it quick by hammering more nails into di old zinc. But mi aunt, who people tease as "coco head" because she was slow with book learning, stop him. She suggested patch it with tar and board instead of driving in more nails. At first he laughed, but when he finally tried it, the roof held steady whole season. Madda smile and say, *"Two head betta dan one, even if a coco head. Wisdom nuh hide in fancy talk alone, sometimes it come from unexpected voice."*

"Empty bag cyaan stan up." Strength need substance. Just like sack need filling, the body need food, and the spirit need truth. Hungry people quickly fall under the weight of life. Fill yuhself with learning, faith, and resilience.

"Ben di tree while it young, when it ole it haard fi bruk!" Early discipline easier than late correction. Mi madda was strict, not out of cruelty, but out of foresight. She seh, "Better bend now than break later." Early discipline easier than late correction, habits formed young last a lifetime. And truly, those habits formed young still carry me today.

"Shut mout nuh ketch fly." Mi madda always warn us that silence is golden. Words, once let loosed, cyaan tek back, and often bring more trouble than peace. She seh, *"Better fi hold yuh tongue and keep yuh dignity than fi loose it and lose yuh way, because loose lips sink ship."*

I remember when two neighbors started quarrelling in di lane, each shouting louder than the next. One turn to Madda, expecting her to take side. But Madda just keep folding clothes, humming softly. Later she tell us, *"See how mi quiet? Mi mout nah ketch fly."* Before long, the quarrel done, while those who argued still carry the shame.

Wisdom whisper where noise confuse. Patience carry yuh farther than pride. Preparation shield yuh long before battle call. Mi madda's wisdom string these truths together like beads on one cord, restraint, foresight, endurance. True resilience is not in strength alone, but in di quiet choices dat save face, build tomorrow, and carry us steady up life hill.

"Wisdom may guard yuh steps, but it is people and fate dat test di journey."

Chapter 9

Community and Survival

A s mi madda use to seh, *"Life is one big market, everybody sell, everybody buy, but not everybody honest."* Human nature is a strange mix: loyalty and betrayal, greed and generosity, laughter, and sorrow. Fate may set the stage, but it is people, our choices, our relationships, our character, that decide how the play ends. Her proverbs were not just sayings; they were compass points to guide us through the crowd of life.

"If yuh nuh mash ant you nuh know him gut." Until pressure squeeze a man, yuh cyan know him true inside. Plenty people smile in calm weather but show temper when storm come. Madda reminded me not to judge too early. She seh, *"Watch how dem act when dem foot mash."* True enough, hardship reveal character more than ease.

"What sweet a mout, hot a belly." Not everything that feel good now will be good later.. Pleasure today can turn sorrow tomorrow. Temporary pleasure often carry regret. Whether it's food, words, or quick gain, what please today can punish tomorrow.

"Hog nyam weh him mine give him fah." Greed carry consequence. A pig eat and eat until him own belly destroy him. *"Feast today and famine tomorrow."* Madda warn: *"Too much self-interest is self-destruction."* It remind me of people who tek bribe fi short gain but lose respect forever.

"Wha di goat do, di kid fallah." Children follow example, not lecture because "pickney eyes sharper than pickney ears." Mi madda seh, *"If yuh want yuh child walk straight, fix yuh own foot first."* Every Sunday morning Mass Johnny polish his shoes, press his shirt, and gather his Bible under arm. His little daughter watch him carefully, then run inside to fetch her own tiny Bible and sit beside him on the step, legs swinging. Har madda smile wide and say, *"Wha di goat do, di kid fallah. Set good path, an' di young will walk it too."*

Just as bad habits pass down, so do good ones. A life of discipline, kindness, and faith echo into the next generation.

"Birds of a fedda flock togedda" and "If yuh lie wid dwag, yuh rise wid flee."
Mi madda always seh, *"Yuh company shape yuh destiny, for who yuh walk wid rub off pon yuh."* Influence rub off fast, and stain spread quick. Good or bad, yuh spirit attract di same spirit.

I saw it plain wid a girl at school, bright, respectful, but always wid company known fi gossip and trouble. Soon teacher dem start eye her same way, whether guilty or not. By the time she realized, the mark already tek hold.

76

She remind us that influence cut both ways. If yuh walk wid people of discipline, yuh pick up discipline. Walk wid reader, yuh hand soon find book. Walk wid liar, yuh tongue soon move same way. In other words, choose circle like yuh choose food, for both nourish or poison di body.

"Yuh cyaan plant corn and expect peas." Actions bring consequence. Mi madda always seh, *"Life give yuh back what yuh put in."* Just like field, corn seed bring corn stalk, pea seed bring pea vine. Yuh cyaan live careless and expect wise result. I remember one youth in di lane who spend him school days skylarking, skipping class, and running domino all afternoon. When exam time come, him bawl because di paper look like another language. Mi madda just shake her head and say, *"Foolish living cyaan yield smart harvest."* Di lesson was clear, effort and action shape the outcome; same way seed decide di crop.

"Every tub haffi siddung pon im own bottom." Responsibility cyaan pass from one to another. Mi schoolmate always try fi blame teacher, friend, even weather for his failure. But at the end of term, the report card carried his name alone. Madda told me plain, "Every tub haffi siddung pon im own bottom." In other words, each life must carry its own weight.

"Cow dead lef trouble fi cow skin." Death neva end responsibility. Burden fall to who left behind, proof that choices outlive us. When uncle pass, di family still haffi bury him, settle debt, raise pickney. Madda seh, "Death close one chapter but open plenty others."

Even so, kinship endure. **"Blood ticka dan wata."** Madda remind mi, *"Friendship come and go, but kinship root strong."* They may quarrel and fight but in our hardest days, it was cousin, sister, aunty who showed up wid pot of food or helping hand.

"Si mi an come live wid mi a two different tings!" Acquaintance nuh equal intimacy. When my cousin moved in with her best friend, within weeks quarrel broke out over dishes, visitors, and noise. The friendship cracked under the weight of daily life. Madda just nod and seh, *"Si mi an come live wid mi a two different tings!"* Not everyone yuh laugh with can share yuh roof.

"Betta people long fi see yuh dan tyad fi see yuh." Mi madda always seh, "Leave room for people to miss yuh." She warn us that too much presence can wear out welcome, even if yuh mean well. Respect nuh only in how yuh show up, but also in knowing when fi step back.

Every evening, Hyacinth come over with story, and sometimes little treat. At first everybody glad fi her company, but after weeks of daily drop-ins, the joy turn to sighs. People start peeping through window, whispering, *"Lawd, she again?"* Mi madda tell us later, *"Betta people long fi see yuh dan tyad fi see yuh. A likkle space sweeten company same way as a likkle salt season pot."*

The wisdom was clear, whether in friendship, family, or love, and balance keep relationships fresh. Presence carry warmth, but absence give it value

"Dawg nyam dawg" Madda seh, "Hard time mek even bredda turn enemy." I remember during one drought; water tank ran dry. Neighbors who once share freely start locking dem gate, guarding barrel like treasure. Quarrels rise over one bucket of water. It was then Madda shake her head: *"See it deh? Dawg nyam dawg. When scarcity bite, kindness shrink."* Survival can bring out both the best and worst in people.

"Dwag nyam you suppa." Mi madda always warn us to guard what we treasure. She told of a neighbor who saved up money fi months, planning fi buy new fridge. Instead of putting it safe, she left it wrapped in a bag on the dresser. One evening, while she was outside chatting, a light-finger cousin passed through and slipped it away. Tears couldn't bring it back. Mi madda only sigh and seh, *"Neglect yuh blessing, anadda mouth claim it."* Lesson? What yuh fail to value or protect, someone else quick fi tek.

"Tief neva like fi see tief carry lang bag." Thief nuh trust thief. Dishonest people quick fi envy one another. Mi madda used to tell a story 'bout two market men who sell yam. One of dem water down the scale, the other mix good yam wid rotten one. Each man know the trick of the other, and neither could stand to see the other prosper. Soon the customers stop coming altogether, nobody trust either stall. Madda would shake her head and seh, *"See? Tief nuh like fi see tief carry lang bag. Crookedness always clash wid crookedness."*

"Bull buck and duppy conqueror." Plenty men talk loud but weak in action. Madda call dem "duppy conqueror", brave when danger far, but trembling when test come close. I remember one youth inna di lane who always boast how him would "tek on any man." But the day a real fight bruk

79

out at the shop, him was the first to run. Mi madda laugh after and seh, *"Bull buck and duppy conqueror, big mouth nuh equal big courage."*

Truth has a way of revealing itself. Mi remember a quarrel in the yard when somebody tief a chicken. Madda neva accuse, she just seh, **"If you fling stone inna hog pen, di first one weh squeal a him it lick."** Sure enough, the loudest protest come from the guilty one, and soon everybody know the truth. *"Guilty conscience make di most noise."*

"Empty barrel mek di most noise." The ones wid di least wisdom often shout di loudest. At market, one woman used to quarrel from sunup to sundown. She argue over price, over space, over anything at all. Yet, her stall never hold goods worth half the noise she made. Mi madda point and whisper, *"Empty barrel mek di most noise."* Words without weight echo loud but hollow.

"Cockroach nuh biznizz eena fowl fight!" Not every fight is yours. If yuh weak, stay out of big man war. Cockroach weh meddle in hen fight only get crush. Not every quarrel is yours to join. I recall one evening when two neighbors clashed over land boundary. Voice raise, stone start fling. A young boy step in fi defend one side, but before him know it, he catch blow that never meant for him. Madda sigh and seh, *"Cockroach nuh biznizz eena fowl fight! Some battle bigger than yuh size, stand back if yuh want live long."*

"A faas mek Anancy deh a house top." Curiosity and meddling carry people where dem nuh belong. Mi madda

always warn, *"Mind yuh own pot, else yuh soup boil over."*
I remember one Sunday when Miss Maizie neighbor nearly
cause pure commotion. She leaned over di fence, eager fi
know why di Johnson yard so quiet. Instead of minding her
pot on di fire, she stretch long, calling, peeping, asking
question. By the time she spin back, di rice bun up black-
bottom. Madda just shake her head and laugh: *"See deh? A
faas mek Anansi deh a house top."* Meaning, when yuh
climb into business dat nuh concern yuh, it only leave yuh
worse off.

"Yuh see today yuh nuh mus see tomorrow." Life fragile,
nothing is guaranteed. Granny would whisper this at
funerals, teaching us to value the present. I recall a
neighbor who spend months planning a "perfect day" fi
celebrate, but while waiting fi tomorrow, today slip away.
Granny always say, *"Treasure di time in front of you, for
tomorrow not promised"*.

Fortune, too, is slippery. **"Horse dead, cow fat."** One
man's loss can become another man's gain. When one shop
in the village close down, the crowd quickly shift to the
competitor across the road. Mi madda would say, *"Horse
dead, cow fat."* Life turn like wheel, today sorrow,
tomorrow feast. She always caution celebrate quietly, for
today's gain, may be tomorrow's grief.

Not every change is improvement. My cousin quit one
miserable job, only to take a worse one, where hours long
and pay short. When she come home crying, Madda just
shake her head and say, ***"Yuh swap black dwag fi
monkey."*** Sometimes we trade trouble fi more trouble,
thinking new always mean better. Wisdom is to look deep

before yuh leap, else yuh leave one pit only to drop in a deeper hole.

"From mi eye de a mi knee." From youth, lessons tek root. Mi madda used to tell us, *"Even from yuh small, yuh learning start."* She loved to recall how as a toddler mi would copy her sweeping yard, broom dragging behind me. Habits form early, for children absorb what they see before they even understand. That's why she always model discipline, knowing little eyes were watching.

"A faithful promise is a comfort to a fool." Empty promise sweet ear, but foolish heart alone believe it. Mi madda often tell of politician who come 'round every four years wid big promises, fix di road, bring water, open job. Villagers clap, sing, and even give him rum. But after election, him vanish like breeze. Madda seh, *"A faithful promise is a comfort to a fool, only action prove word true."*

Mi madda never just teach proverbs, she teach survival wrapped in grace. She'd say: *"Don't just be impressive, be kind. Don't just be smart, be steady. And always know who yuh be, so nobody can sell yuh lie about yuh worth."* Because in di end, name carry weight not because it loud, but because it clean. Connection carry yuh not because it flashy, but because it rooted. And clarity   separate distraction from destiny.

So live so dat yuh presence bring light, and yuh absence leave memory of kindness. Live so yuh children nuh just inherit yuh things, but yuh principles. That is how storm nuh only pass over yuh, but how yuh help others find shelter too.

That is real wealth. That is true resilience.

That is wisdom from Mi Madda.

Final Words
(In the Voice of Mi Madda)

Dis book! It nuh fi collect dust. It live and breathe still, straight from di kitchen talk, di roadside gossip, and di backstep reasoning. Every saying in here? It carry double duty, fi guide and guard, from di days when yuh haffi greet elders proper-proper, "Mawnin' Miss," to di boardroom where integrity still weigh more than big title. So, before yuh close up di pages, come sit likkle. Mek we reason one last time.

First: Hold it inna yuh heart. Mi always tell mi pickney dem: If wisdom only reach yuh ears, it gone same way breeze pass through open window. But, when it drop inna yuh chest and stay deh, ah so change start. "One-one coco full basket" nuh just about patience, it teach yuh how fi build bit by bit, savings, sense, and self. And "Who cyah hear, mus'" feel"? That one grow up wid yuh, start off as scolding, end up as standard. Use di proverbs until caution become habit, until respect come natural, and until thanksgiving meet yuh before coffee.

Second: Speak it out loud. Culture cyah survive in silence. If we nuh talk it, we lose it. So, drop Granny words inna yuh email, inna yuh meeting, or when yuh talking to yuh chile. Stitch dem into everything, di school paper, di church bulletin, di company handbook. Quote Grandpa when yuh tell dem "Waste not, want not," and let "Good fren better dan pocket money" lead yuh mentorship circle. As long as di wisdom travel, even by Wi-Fi, we safe. Di vehicle change, but di message still stand.

Third: Update di meaning but keep di roots. Dem sayings nuh meant fi lock up inna glass case. Dem meant fi grow and stretch. So yes, tek "Pray" and build mindfulness inna yuh policy. Use "Don't licky licky" fi teach boundaries, consent, and data privacy. When yuh warn, "Play wid fire, yuh will get burn," yuh could a be talking 'bout cyber risk or trust breach, it still fit. Di proverb shape-shift, but it nah lose its footing.

Last and always: Big up di matriarchs and di elders. Every lesson dem pass on come wid a price, sometimes a cold pot, sometimes a stifled dream, so yuh could walk free and full. Mek dem proud. Name scholarship after dem. Quote dem in yuh big speeches. And more than all that, live good. Live so solid dem spirit can rest sweet, knowing yuh carry di torch well.

So, listen good. Learn deep. Live wid purpose.

When yuh walk in di words of Mi Madda, yuh don't just preserve old-time wisdom. Yuh push it forward. Yuh turn echo into anthem. And even when our voice done, di melody still play, loud, clear, and everlasting.

Anette Rose White

Proverb Index by Theme

Gratitude and Grounding

- Give thanks for what you have: Gratitude builds contentment.

- Belly full, man tell yuh say fasting good: Privilege forgets hardship.

- He who feels it knows it: Only the one who suffers understands.

- Every mickle mek a muckle: Small blessings add up.

- Tek kin teet cova heartburn: Laughter shields pain.

- Better belly buss than good food waste: Don't waste blessings.

- Di dog with di bone lose di bone: Greed leads to loss.

- Pray: Grounding in faith before all things.

- Leave it to God: Trust divine timing and justice.

- Mi nuh eat from everybody kitchen: Discernment and boundaries.

- Dog that bring a bone carry one: Gossipers can't be trusted.

- Rain nuh fall pon one man house: Trouble spares no one.

- Every lizard lay down pon dem belly: Appearances don't reveal struggle.

- Treat man good pan bottom: Kindness when others are down.

- Forgive but don't forget: Release pain, keep wisdom.

- Don't cut off yuh nose to spite yuh face: Don't let pride ruin peace.

- Dis day cyah hol' di nex: Don't carry yesterday into tomorrow.

- First time is a mistake; second time is purpose: Repeated error is choice.

- Long run, short ketch: Consequences always catch up.

- Time longer than rope: Patience brings justice.

- What is done in darkness will come to light: Truth will be revealed.

- If fish come from river bottom an' tell yuh say shark down deh, believe him: Respect lived experience.

- Tek weh yuh get til you get weh yuh want: Contentment as steppingstone.

- No wait till drum beat before yuh grine yuh axe: Prepare before crisis.

- When man belly full, him tink a starvation time: Comfort breeds forgetfulness.

Grace Before Greatness

- Be kind to others: Kindness is non-negotiable.

- Don't meet bad wid bad. Kill dem wid kindness: Grace in action.

- Kindness and good manners will get you through the world.

- Do unto others as you would have them do to you.

- Yuh cyah tek back spit: Words once spoken cannot be undone.

- Yuh cyah climb ladder wid han' inna yuh pocket: Progress requires effort.

- Graveyard full a people who feel important: Pride is fleeting.

- Saying good morning to everyone who cross yuh path: Manners are dignity.

- Respect your elders.

- Howdy and tenky nuh bruk no square: Courtesy smooths relations.

- Children should be seen and not heard.

- Stay outta big people business.

- High seat kill Miss Thomas puss: Pride leads to downfall.

- Mi come yah fi drink milk, mi nuh come fi kill cow: Know your purpose.

- A soft answer turns away wrath.

- People who live in a glass house don't throw stone.: Warning against hypocrisy.

- If you spit in the sky it will fall in your eye.: Actions rebound.

- Pig ask him mumma, 'Mumma, how yuh mouth suh long?' Mumma say, 'Wait, yuh time coming.': Age brings perspective.

- Yuh cyah swear fi heart when face still smile: Smiles can deceive.

- Stick to yuh stick inna bush: Stay loyal to roots.

Wisdom in Proverbs

- One-one coco full basket: Patience builds success.

- Not everything good fi eat good fi talk: Discretion matters.

- No mek yuh lef' hand know what yuh right hand a do: Move wisely, silently.

- Cock mout kill cock.: Loose talk brings ruin.

- Wall have ears.

- Mouth open, story jump out.

- Silent riva run deep.: Quiet people hold wisdom.

- A see you cyan see, or a nah see you nah see: Discernment goes beyond sight.

- A nuh every shut eye mean sleep.: Awareness hides in stillness.

- A nuh who you see, a who see you.: You are always being observed.

- Don't tek man fi fool just because him quiet.

- Trouble mek monkey eat pepper.: Foolishness leads to suffering.

- Rockstone a river bottom nuh know sun hot.: Sheltered people misunderstand struggle.

- Ananc know which leaf fi hide under.: Cleverness survives.

- Scornful dawg nyam dutty pudden.: Don't despise humble things.

- Never look a gift horse in the mouth.

- Empty barrel mek di most noise.: Boastfulness without substance.

- Stick bruk inna yuh eaz?: Ignoring advice brings consequences.

- Wanti wanti cyah getti, and getti getti nuh wanti.: Irony of desire.

- What eye don't see, heart don't leap.: Ignorance can bring peace.

- New broom sweep clean, but old broom know di corner.: Respect for both youth and age.

- Every day bucket go a well, one day di bottom will drop out.: Habits collapse eventually.

- Too much rat nah mek dog sleep.: Constant stress robs peace.

- Self-praise is no recompense.

- If ah did know, dog nyam yuh supper.: Regret too late.

- Waste not, want not.: Frugality preserves.

- What sweet yuh gwine sour yuh.: Pleasures turn sour.

- The grass is not always greener on the other side.

- Respect your elders. (appears here too; indexed once under Grace)

- Frog seh, what is joke to you is death to me.: Sensitivity differs.

- Not all that glitter is gold.

- Good friend better than pocket money.: Friendship as currency.

- Money mek fren, and money bruk fren.

- Don't lend more than you can afford to lose.

- Look before you leap.

- Every hoe have him stick a bush.: Everyone has a match.

- Not everything you want is good for you.

- Too many cooks spoil the broth.

Iron Sharpens Iron

- Who cyah hear, mus' feel.: Disobedience leads to consequence.

- Learn from your mistake.

- No mek di same stick lick yuh two time.: Don't repeat errors.

- Hard ears pickney dead a sun hot.: Stubbornness destroys.

- If you want good, yuh nose haffi run.: Effort brings reward.

- Practice mek perfect.

- Jackass seh di worl' nuh level, an' him back prove it.: Hardship proves inequality.

- Sleep and mark death.: Laziness invites downfall.

- No wait till yuh thirsty fi dig well.: Prepare early.

- Tek yuh hand an' tun fashion.: Resourcefulness creates solutions.

Character and Connection

- One han' cyaan clap.: Community is essential.

- Good fren' come from hard times.

- Every smile nuh mean teeth clean.: Appearances deceive.

- Same knife stick sheep stick goat.: Betrayal from close hands.

- No call di piper till di dance done.: Don't judge prematurely.

- Ants follow fat, not promise.: Actions, not words, attract.

- Stone inna mango tree mean mango ripe.: Signs point to truth.

- Backra massa days done.: Old oppression is past.

Fate, Effort, and Consequence

- What is fi yuh cyaan be un-fi yuh.: Destiny cannot be denied.

- No put yuh basket weh yuh cyaan reach it.: Don't overreach.

- Rain a fall, but dutty tough.: Resilience despite hardship.

- Tek sleep mark death.: Small signs foreshadow.

- Time longer than rope. (also, in Gratitude; indexed once).

Wisdom and Warnings

- Chicken merry, hawk deh near.: Joy and danger walk together.

- Cockroach nuh business inna fowl fight.: Stay out of others' conflict.

- Fire deh a muss-muss tail.: Trouble hidden will burn.

- Play wid puppy, puppy lick yuh mouth.: Play leads to consequence.

- Play wid fire, yuh will get burn.: Recklessness invites harm.

- Sickness is no respecter of persons.: Illness spares no one.

Prudence, Patience, and Preparedness

- Finga neva seh look here, him seh look deh.

- If you han inna debil mout, tek time draw it out.

- Nuh wait til drum beat to grine yu axe.

- Coward man keep sound bone.

- Patient man ride donkey.

- Pound a fret cyan pay ounce a debt.

- Nuh buy puss inna bag.

- Shoes alone know if stocking have hole.

- Small axe chop big tree.

- Humble calf suck di most milk.

- If yuh nuh done climb hill, nuh dash weh yuh stick.

- Monkey muss know weh him gwine put him tail before him orda troussers.

- Nuh count yuh chicken before dem hatch.

- A bird in the hand is worth two in di bush.

- Shut mout nuh ketch fly.

- Suck salt outta wooden spoon.

- Too much a one ting good fi nutten.

- Two head betta dan one, even if a coco head.

- Empty bag cyan stan up.

- Ben di tree while it young, wen it ole it haad fi bruk.

Community and Survival

- If yuh nuh mash ant, yuh nuh know him gut.

- What sweet a mout, hot a belly.

- Hog nyam weh him mine give him fah.

- Wha di goat do, di kid falla.

- A faas mek Anancy deh a house top.

- A faithful promise is a comfort to a fool.

- Blood ticka dan wata.

- Birds of a feada flock togedda.

- Cow dead lef trouble fi cow skin.

- Dawg nyam dawg.

- Dwag nyam yuh suppa.

- Empty barrel mek di most noise.

- Every tub haffi siddung pon im own bottom.

- From mi eye de a mi knee.

- From salfish a shingle roof.

- Horse dead, cow fat.

- If you fling stone inna hog pen, di first one weh squeal a him it lick.

- If yuh lie wid dwag, yuh rise wid flea.

- Tief neva like fi see tief carry lang bag.

- Bull buck and duppy conqueror.

- Yuh cyan plant corn and expect peas.

- Yuh see today, yuh nuh mus see tomorrow.

- Yuh swap black dwag fi monkey.

- Si mi an come live wid mi a two different tings!

- Cockroach nuh biznizz eena fowl fight!

Anette Rose White

Glossary of Jamaican Words

Word / Expression	Definition / Usage
ah / a	Is or it is. Common verb marker in patois. Example: A nuh every shut eye mean sleep. (Not every closed eye means someone is asleep; appearances deceive.)
Anansi	Trickster figure in African and Caribbean folklore, often a spider; symbol of cunning and curiosity.
backra / backra massa	Historically, a term for European slave masters; by extension, symbolizes colonial oppression. Rare in modern speech, but still used proverbially. Example: Backra massa days done. (The days of colonial masters are over.)
belly	Stomach; also used figuratively to mean courage, appetite, or inner strength.

big up	To praise, show respect, or greet warmly. Used as everyday greeting or farewell. Example: Big up yuhself, mi fren. (Respect to you, my friend.)
bredda	Brother; can mean a male sibling or close male friend.
bruk	To break; also means broke (without money). Example: Mi shoe bruk up. (My shoe is broken.)
buss	To burst, break open; also, to laugh loudly or succeed. Example: Better belly buss than good food waste. (Better to overeat than waste food.)
bush	Countryside, rural area, or wild vegetation.
calf	Young cow; symbolizes humility or inexperience. Example: Humble calf suck di most milk.
cyaa / cyaan / cyah	Cannot. Variant spellings, very common. Example: Who cyaan hear, mus' feel.

	(Those who won't listen must feel the consequences.)
cyaan bodda	Can't be bothered. Everyday expression of annoyance or fatigue. Example: Mi cyaan bodda wid dat today. (I can't be bothered with that today.)
cock mout	Loose talk, reckless speech. Example: Cock mout kill cock. (Loose talk brings ruin.)
coco head	A playful or insulting term for someone seen as slow-witted or simple-minded.
come live wid mi	To move in and share space with someone; proverbially highlights the difference between casual acquaintance and true intimacy.
coward man	One who avoids conflict or danger; proverbially seen as wise for surviving. Example: Coward man keep sound bone.
dawg / dwag	Dog.

deh	There. Example: Book deh pon table. (The book is on the table.)
dem	Them. Plural marker. Example: Mi see dem yesterday. (I saw them yesterday.)
duppy	Ghost or spirit. Duppy conqueror refers to someone who talks tough but folds under pressure.
dutty	Dirty; also means stubborn, hardened, or tough. Example: Rain a fall, but dutty tough. (Rain falls, but hardship continues.)
falla	To follow. In proverbs, often warns that children imitate what they see.
fi	To, for, or of (possessive). Example: Fi mi madda. (My mother.)
fi mek	In order to, for the sake of. Example: Tek kin teet fi mek heartburn hide. (Use laughter to cover pain.)
finga	Finger; used proverbially to mean guidance or quiet

direction. Example: Finga neva seh look here, him seh look deh.

fret — Worry, anxiety.

granny / gran' — Grandmother, elder. Used with affection and respect.

grine — Grind, sharpen, prepare. Example: Nuh wait till drum beat to grine yuh axe. (Prepare before crisis come.)

gut — Belly or insides. Figuratively means inner truth revealed under pressure.

haffi — Have to, must. Example: If yuh want good, yuh nose haffi run. (If you want good things, you must work hard.)

han' — Hand. Example: One han' cyaan clap. (Community is essential.)

hill — Hill or mountain; represents struggle, journey, or achievement.

jackass	Donkey; symbolizes hardship, foolishness, or burden. Example: Jackass seh di worl' nuh level, an' him back prove it.
kibba	To cover or hide. Example: Tek kin teet kibba heartburn. (Use laughter to cover pain.)
lick	To hit or strike. Example: Nuh mek di same stick lick yuh two time.
licky licky	Greedy, eager for food or favors.
likkle	Little. Example: Mi likkle but mi tallawah. (I am small but mighty.)
long fi see yuh	To miss someone, to wish for their presence.
madda	Mother
mawga	Thin, weak, emaciated. Example: Sorry fi mawga dawg, him run come bite yuh.
mek	To make, let, or allow. Example: Every mickle mek a muckle. (Every little adds up to a lot.)

mi	Me, my. First-person pronoun. Example: Mi come yah fi drink milk, mi nuh come fi count cow.
mout / mout'	Mouth; refers to speech, talk, or words.
mussi / muss	Must, have to.
nuh	Not, don't, or no.
nyam	To eat. Common verb.
pickney	Child or children.
puppy	Young dog; figuratively, naive or overly familiar person. Example: Play wid puppy, puppy lick yuh mouth.
puss	Cat. Often used in proverbs about pride or deception.
quakoo / quako	Placeholder name for somebody, like "John Doe."
seh	Say.
set / tek set	To target or single out. Example: Trouble nuh set like rain. (Trouble comes unexpectedly.)

shut eye	Closed eyes; figuratively means pretending not to see.
sorry fi	To pity.
suppa	Supper, evening meal.
tallawah	Strong, fearless, resilient despite small size. Beloved Jamaican self-description.
teet	Teeth. Figuratively, laughter. Example: Tek kin teet kibba heartburn. (Use laughter to cover pain.)
tek	To take. Examples: Tek weh yuh get til yuh get weh yuh want. (Be content until better comes.) Tek sleep mark death. (Learn from small signs.)
ting	Thing.
tink	Think.
tyad	Tired, weary.
waan / wan	Want, or one.
walk good	A farewell blessing, meaning "go safely."
weh	What, where. Example: Weh yuh deh? (Where are you?)

weh mek	Why; literally, "what make." Example: Weh mek yuh late? (Why are you late?)
wi / we	We, our, us.
yuh	You, your.
zinc	Corrugated metal sheet used for roofing.

Anette Rose White

Acknowledgments

Giving thanks is more than manners, it is memory. It is standing still long enough to recognize the hands that held you up, the hearts that poured into you, and the voices that whispered keep going when your own breath was short.

To my mother, mi madda, whose wisdom, wit, and unwavering faith shaped the soul of this book. You didn't just raise children, you raised thinkers, dreamers, and doers. Every proverb in these pages carries your voice, and every lesson echoes your love.

To my family, especially my children, Kitanya and Gloriana, thank you for being my daily reminders of purpose and perseverance. Your laughter and resilience breathe life into everything I write.

To Thomas, thank you for your love, your encouragement, and your quiet strength. You make the hard days easier and the good days even sweeter.

To my sister, Teckla, who always there to listening, remembering, and helping me remember the stories and sayings that might have slipped away. Your presence is a quiet, steady gift I treasure more than you know.

To the aunties, uncles, neighbors, and church elders whose sayings and stories embroidered my upbringing, you didn't just teach me how to survive; you taught me how to live with dignity and humor.

To my community of readers, students, and clients, thank you for reminding me that these words still matter. You are proof that ancestral wisdom never expires.

National Library of Jamaica (NLJ) – Guardian of Jamaica's documentary heritage and a vital source for preserving and promoting Jamaican proverbs, folklore, and cultural traditions.

To Jamaica, my first classroom, my first rhythm, my first root. Dis book a fi yuh.

And above all, to the Creator who guides my pen, guards my path, and grants grace even when mi steps crooked, tanks.

Walk good,

Anette

About the Author

Anette Rose White is a certified professional coach, human resource professional, educator, and transformational leader whose passion for empowerment is deeply rooted in her Jamaican heritage. As the founder and CEO of Anette R Coaching, she equips young adults and professionals with the essential life skills, mindset, and clarity needed to thrive through life's transitions. Drawing on over two decades of experience in corporate human resources, Anette bridges the gap between personal growth and real-world readiness.

Raised in Kingston, Jamaica WI, and deeply influenced by the rich oral traditions of her upbringing, Anette blends ancestral wisdom with modern insight. *Wisdom from Mi Madda* is both a tribute and a legacy, an intergenerational gift that captures the strength, humor, and values passed down through time-honored proverbs and heartfelt reflections from her mother.

Anette holds certifications from the International Coaching Federation (ICF) and is a celebrated speaker, workshop facilitator, and community advocate. Her life's work centers on helping others rise above limitations, discover their purpose, and walk boldly in their truth, with grace, confidence, and a touch of island flair.

When she's not coaching, writing, or speaking, Anette enjoys traveling, photography, spending time with her family, and savoring a cold glass of Jamaican sorrel.

Anette Rose White

www.ingramcontent.com/pod-product-compliance
Lightning Source LLC
Chambersburg PA
CBHW052038270326
41931CB00012B/2543